The Led Zeppelin Curse

Jimmy Page and the Haunted
Boleskine House

-By Lance Gilbert

Published by Lance Gilbert
Email: lancea.gilbert@hotmail.com
Cover Idea: Lance Gilbert
ISBN 978-0-473-41053-7

First Edition
© Copyright Lance Gilbert 2017

Contents

Preface

Rock music has always had a way of inciting youthful passion. Led Zeppelin has a way of inciting multigenerational passion in a torrent of endless, hypnotic waves. The tsunami of Zeppelin makes its way across the globe again and again, building year after year; but why? What about this band in particular creates such an intense fervor?

Since the late 70's, following a string of accidents, mayhem and death, there has been talk of a Led Zeppelin Curse. Sure; many rock bands have seen their fair share of tragedy. Fast living, money, fame and drugs are a combustible mixture and it's no surprise when one of the houses in that neighborhood is ablaze. When you play with fire anything can happen. When you play with the occult those flames cannot be subdued with water alone. What exactly is a curse? Loosely defined; a curse is a solemn utterance intended to invoke a supernatural power to inflict harm or punishment on someone or something.

Jimmy Page was indeed publicly cursed by a rather ferocious wizard. But can the existence of a curse be definitively proven? Was Led Zeppelin's downfall the result of a specific curse thrown at them, Jimmy Page's longtime general interest in the occult or a combination thereof? Many Zeppelin fans think the curse is nonsense and perhaps it is. Regardless, Page's fascination with magick and infamous Victorian era magician Aleister Crowley in particular makes this a tantalizing trail to follow. As they say, the Devil is in the details.

In early November of 2015 I was finishing up my second book on the occult & paranormal. As part of a chapter on unique haunted locations I wrote about Boleskine House (boll-ESS-kin) which was owned by Jimmy Page for almost twenty two years. Page bought the manor because it was previously inhabited by the aforementioned occultist Aleister Crowley. Boleskine House, located on the southeast side of Loch Ness in the Scottish Highlands, had quite a history of its own before Crowley or Page ever set foot in it and we'll swim through those waters later.

In late November I posted an excerpt from my haunted locations chapter in various paranormal and Led Zeppelin Facebook groups. The response was amazing; people definitely had an opinion about the occult / Jimmy Page connection. I also learned the true extent of Zeppelin's popularity, the intensity of their fan base and of the curious segment of followers that become quite agitated when there is any mention of Jimmy Page and the occult. I kept joining related groups and posting the excerpt as I planned to circle back and promote in those groups again after the book was complete.

Then in late December someone sent me a link to a BBC story. Boleskine House was on fire! By no means am I implying that my postings had somehow triggered this blaze but I took it as a sign. Perhaps there was a book here. A chance to write about and tie in multiple subjects that fascinated me was very exciting. Rock music's connection to the occult, Jimmy Page and Aleister Crowley, a possible curse and of course the eerie Boleskine House were all topics that set me on fire. The seeds were sown for my next writing project.

I am not a Led Zeppelin fan in the literal sense. I am not fanatical about them. I do like their music and certain songs are on my play-lists, etc. If anything, this allows me to be more objective as I don't think this kind of book can be properly written without a bit of space; a healthy distance from the mania that is Zeppelin. My connection is the occult angle. I've had extensive, direct experience with the occult and in particular the type of practice that Aleister Crowley (and possibly Jimmy Page) engaged in while living at Boleskine House.

During my reckless youth I attempted to summon the very same demonic forces that Crowley supposedly unleashed at Loch Ness. Please be aware that I'm very careful about making declarative statements in regards to the paranormal or anything else for that matter. There's nothing more irritating than someone with a know-it-all tone so if you pick up on that at any point in this book it's not my intention. If there's one thing I definitely know it's that I don't know anything for sure. It's impossible to prove the supernatural in a 3rd dimensional context and it would be a waste of time to even attempt. However, like Jimmy Page, I was also obsessed with Crowley and one of the zones where it all overlaps is the haunted Boleskine House.

When the idea to explore the legend of the Zeppelin Curse first hit me I asked myself what value I could add. After all; many books have been written about this musical behemoth so what else could possibly be revealed? The late 60's and the entirety of the 70's were Led Zeppelin's heyday. But let's face it; memory is consistent...consistently unreliable. Add the haze of drugs and hysteria that surrounds superstardom and you've got a recipe for half-truths and hyperbole. The three to four decade old drug and alcohol clouded recollections of insiders are fascinating and have their place in the Zeppelin pantheon but will we ever get the truth? Does truth even exist? The point is that it's not as much about the so-called facts but how they are tied together and interpreted. My direct experience with the occult and supernatural will allow me to shed light on this mystery in a way that hasn't been presented before.

The fact that Jimmy Page himself has always remained sheepishly quiet about his occult practice is a smoking gun for me. Shall we look down that barrel and see what's really there? We're going to have to because cagey Pagey, as he's often called, will never tell us. He's quite a private man and has every right to be given that the vulture of fame can pick one's bones clean in the blink of an eye. Jimmy Page may or may not have practiced occult rituals but whether or not he was working magick I do believe that magick was working on Led Zeppelin. But was it white magick, black magick or something else? Perhaps it doesn't make a difference considering that simplistic labels like black and white are irrelevant.

Earlier I mentioned that the Zeppelin fan base covers an unusually broad age demographic. This can also be said for the fascinating cross section of individuals that wave the banner of this iconic British super group. There are the Crowleyites who, like Jimmy Page, follow the work and teachings of 19th century occultist and renaissance man (of sorts) Aleister Crowley. Then there are the pagans, mystics and hippies who passionately resonate with Zeppelin's folk influences. And of course we have the guitarists who appreciate Page's work as a pre-Zeppelin studio musician / session's man and the dragon suit wearing god he would later become.

There are many other types of Zeppelin fans but the reason I address this is due to the intense divide I ran into when posting the aforementioned Boleskine House-related book excerpts starting in November of 2015. There were fans that were open to the magick / occult angle and those who were definitely not. Wow; I guess I should have expected it given my years of experience with debating the paranormal. The overriding message from the non-believers was 'enough of the hocus pocus; let's concentrate on the music', etc. But why the resistance when Jimmy Page is a self-avowed practitioner of Crowley's magical systems? Why such opposition when there is irrefutable evidence of occult symbolism and practice with Page?

I will not be attempting to convince anyone of anything. We are all on our own trip and we all perceive the world differently and everyone's point of view has validity to it. My background is the occult so I'll be looking through that particular lens. However; I want to include all Zeppelin fans so let's make a deal, ok? If you are completely against or very doubtful of the whole occult / Crowley connection and think it's absolute nonsense I want you to do something. Just suspend your disbelief and enjoy the ride. We all do that when watching movies, right?

If Jimmy Page wasn't into the occult I wouldn't have written this book. People can ignore and/or disagree with that part of the band's past but it's still there; it's still a part of Zeppelin whether they think its BS or not. A review of my second book comes to mind in regards to addressing nonbelievers. This sums it up pretty well...

'While I don't agree with all of the conclusions reached in the book, it is well written. I have a habit of correcting the grammatical errors in books because some of them drive me crazy and this book has remarkably few corrections. I am giving it only 4 stars because it left me wanting more information. I want to hear more stories of actual cases and how they were dealt with. It was certainly not dry or boring. If you don't like a sort of stream of consciousness style of writing, you may not like this book. If you need absolute proof in order to think of something as valid, you may not like this book. If you don't like reading about opinions that are not mainstream, you may not like this book. If, however, you don't mind these things, you should give this book a read. I don't have to agree with someone's every thought to appreciate where they are coming from. Overall, I'm glad I read this book. It has, at least, given me something new to consider.'

That's exactly it; I'd like to give you something new to consider or at least a different take on what you're already familiar with.

If you are among the anti-occult Zeppelin fans I still invite you to come along on this journey and give it some consideration without the knee-jerk reaction. You'll have to accept and maybe even embrace the fact that the occult influenced their music. Perhaps this part of the band's history was never presented to you correctly. I will endeavor to do just that- then you can take it or leave it.

However, if you're not able to put your resistance to the occult connections aside then this probably isn't the book for you. I'd rather have an open-minded person enjoy this story and know what they're getting into before investing any more time. We will be talking about all sorts of intangible stuff like spirits, energy and magick. I'll present some theories you might find outrageous; blasphemous even. If that's not your cup of tea or you can't at least entertain the idea of such things then turn back now.

By no means am I saying that I think Jimmy Page is a Devil worshipper or a Satanist. Those rather unfortunate trigger words create a smokescreen obscuring the real story. However, there is sufficient evidence that he has practiced magick rituals in one form or another and applied this (to some degree) to his recorded music and performances as a member of Led Zeppelin. Page has gone on record to this effect and has also stated that he utilizes a 'magical system' espoused by occultist Aleister Crowley.

There is also solid evidence that Jimmy Page was cursed by underground film maker and fellow Aleister Crowley enthusiast Kenneth Anger back in 1976 after a row over a soundtrack Page was supposed to deliver for one of Anger's films.

Jimmy Page strongly downplays his occult interest despite having let enough corroborative info slip in interviews over the years. I'm sure that many if not most of his old buddies will be on the same page when recalling that time period; at least when it comes to the occult. People close to the rich and famous often tow the line to stay in the good books. I could be wrong but that is definitely something to consider when you hear 'insiders' proclaim that Jimmy only researched the occult but never practiced it. Please also bear in mind that there is a great deal of conflicting information about the group online and just because something is repeated often doesn't make it so.

With the above in mind, this book is a combination of information, interpretation and speculation. Hardcore Zeppelin fanatics have already come across much of this info but will find the interpretation and speculation of interest; particularly my conclusions regarding who or what may be responsible for this curse. Casual Zeppelin fans may have heard bits and pieces of the legend but will likely enjoy getting a fuller picture here. Paranormal and occult enthusiasts will surely appreciate the haunted Boleskine House and Aleister Crowley angles.

The story of the Led Zeppelin Curse didn't just appear in a poof of smoke. However, Jimmy Page himself once said when asked about his reputation, 'where there's smoke there's usually fire.' With that typically cryptic statement from Page in mind, please consider the possibility that everything you thought was Zeppelin gospel might just have a different twist depending on the source of information.

Throughout this book I'll sometimes refer to Jimmy Page as JP and Aleister Crowley as AC to spare you the repetition which might disrupt the flow of the story. I'll also refer to magic as 'magick' depending on the context as Aleister Crowley has altered the spelling to differentiate the magic tricks of an illusionist versus ritual magicians who allegedly use their will to affect physical reality. There will be some humor too. Please don't mistake an occasionally jocular tone as lack of respect for the subject matter. On the contrary; this is dangerous stuff and levity keeps the demonic at bay.

Here we go- jump in with me and let's steep in the Zeppelin universe.

Introduction

The legend of the Led Zeppelin Curse emerged in the late 1970's after multiple accidents and deaths plagued the band and/or those close to them. Many have suggested that Jimmy Page's intense interest in the occult and in particular the notorious Edwardian magician Aleister Crowley is to blame. However, the curse itself refers to both the bad luck the band experienced as well as a specific curse put upon Jimmy Page by avant-garde film maker and occultist Kenneth Anger. Page and Anger's paths crossed as a result of their mutual interest in Crowley.

The guitar itself has quite a history when it comes to the supernatural. Jimmy Page is a big fan of 1930's American Blues musician Robert Johnson. Supposedly Johnson once stood at the crossroads of Highways 49 and 61 in Clarksdale, Mississippi and sold his soul to the Devil in exchange for guitar-playing prowess. However, this legend goes back even further to the 1920's with various black musicians and gamblers signing a pact with a supernatural-type character at the crossroads. This allegedly all originates with the slaves in the American south and the magic they brought from overseas. Of course this is all just a legend but as the old saying goes, where there's smoke there's fire.

Following on from the Robert Johnson story there has long been talk that the members of Led Zeppelin (minus pragmatic bassist John Paul Jones), at the behest of Jimmy Page, had engaged in a pact with the Devil, selling their souls for fame and fortune. Most of this pact with the Devil talk came to the forefront after John Bonham choked on his own vomit and died in late September of 1980. The media seized on JP's well-known occult interest and suggested that all of his dabbling was to blame which of course royally pissed him off.

There have been many books written about Led Zeppelin. Most are good, thorough accounts by those close to the band. However, there hasn't been much which specifically focuses on Jimmy Page's obsession with Aleister Crowley and the occult, his purchase of and experiences in Boleskine House and the curse laid on him by Kenneth Anger. With a name like that it sounds as if he'd be someone to throw curses, right? Due to my previous experiences with the occult, this particular sub-story in the Zeppelin saga is one I can shed some light on.

We'll explore Jimmy Page's introduction to Aleister Crowley's work and how it turned into a full-blown lifetime obsession. If Page hadn't run into one of Crowley's books as a youngster we probably wouldn't be having this chat. The controversial magician himself with be discussed as we weave Page's history into Crowley's, all culminating in their meeting (albeit on different timelines) at the haunted Boleskine House. Crowley brought the Devil, quite literally, to the Scottish Highlands and created a legend which reverberates to this day. The old manor on the Loch is a character unto itself and we'll dig into its history of death, fires and the demonic.

Houses are living breathing things and Boleskine has dark memories and sharp teeth. Jimmy Page couldn't help but inject his music (both recorded and live) with magick and occult symbolism and we'll get into those particulars including Crowley's phrases actually being pressed into Zeppelin albums! The band's well-known use of magical symbols will also be explored including Jimmy Page's concert garb which was adorned with ancient occultic references. Were Zeppelin concerts magical rituals and did the after-show groupie sex-fests complete the ceremonies? Ridiculous, you say? Read on and consider what's presented before making any snap judgments.

The curse itself will be examined including a bit of history on the intense and often frightening Kenneth Anger who was so...well...angry at JP that he launched a campaign of focused malevolence at the famous guitarist. There is more to a curse's effectiveness than just death and maiming. Sometimes there are things that are not reported in the media, things that happen behind the scenes which have cumulative effects and are just as awful as the more dramatic occurrences one might expect.

Curiously enough, the Zeppelin did indeed start to plummet after Anger's curse. I'm not necessarily saying that his mental venom was responsible for the band's slow motion crash but we'll have a look at the series of events and then decide whether or not there's any merit in blaming the boogeyman. It's also quite possible that Page's occult dabbling, unrelated to Kenneth Anger, might have caused a chain reaction which may (and I stress may) have led to the band's premature end.

Since drummer John Bonham's death there has been constant talk of Led Zeppelin reunions and/or reformations. Nothing significant ever materialized and at the time of this writing it looks like they will never get back together. We'll talk about the potential reasons for why the three surviving band members, along with Bonham's son Jason (also a drummer) haven't gone back on the road to relive the old glory and cash in on a billion-dollar payday.

Of course I will share my conclusions as culpability must be assigned following this investigation. I think you'll be surprised by what I arrive at and more so the specific historical tie in I reference to make my case.

Our last chapter will cover Boleskine House's unfortunate demise in December of 2015. There will also be discussion around Loch Ness itself and whether or not Aleister Crowley's dark rituals opened a permanent doorway which

Jimmy Page stepped through when he bought the haunted manor. Crazy, you say? Yes, it does sound like a bit of a stretch but there are some interesting correlations which will give us food for thought because Loch Ness is known for more than just Crowley, Page and Boleskine House.

Here we go...remember, this book is for entertainment. I seek to prove nothing except to share my take on an interesting story. As Ripley says, you can believe it or not. And for the record, this has not been authorized by Jimmy Page or any of the remaining members of Led Zeppelin. No surprise there, right?

1 Crowley's Page

Just about everyone has heard of Jimmy Page; the iconic guitarist of Led Zeppelin that lived like a god through the 70's. But not everyone knew of his fascination with the occult and in particular with the notorious and (depending on who you're talking to) misunderstood Edwardian era magician Aleister Crowley. Yes, many musicians of that time period flirted with the dark side and even reveled in it as a prop of sorts. However, none were as dedicated to studying just what could be done with the ancient science of magick as James Patrick Page.

Crowley himself was quite the enigma. Known mainly as a dark occultist, his other talents and interests were obscured by his outer personae as an evil magician. He was also an artist, poet, novelist and accomplished mountaineer among other things. It is also said that he was recruited by British intelligence and participated in an occult disinformation plot against the Nazis.

We'll dip into Crowley a bit more soon enough but for those that don't know much about him this will give you a sense of the scope of his influence. At the personal request of John Lennon, Crowley's image found its way onto the cover of the Beatles' Sergeant Pepper album. Check it out- he's in the back on the left between Mae West and an Indian guru. Crackpot afterthoughts don't show up on an album that Rolling Stone magazine, in 2003, ranked #1 on its 500 Greatest Albums of All Time list. Crowley died in 1947 when Page was nearly four years old.

Jimmy Page had first been exposed to Aleister Crowley's work around age eleven when he read Magick in Theory and Practice which he stated that he did not fully grasp at the time. It understandably took several years before Page began to understand what it was all about. Regardless, the seeds were sown at an early age and who could have guessed the impact it would ultimately have? Curiously enough, Jimmy Page started playing guitar at age thirteen.

Knowing what we know now; if Page hadn't read Aleister Crowley's book would Led Zeppelin have been the same? A big part of why I started this project is the mystery involved. Page has always been reluctant to discuss his interest in Crowley which makes sense given the controversial subject matter. Throughout the years he has intermittently seemed to open up a bit about this part of his life but ultimately goes quiet; often getting defensive and pissy. This could be in part due to the band's historically rocky relationship with the press who had been quite rough on the group. Page was always suspicious of them and this likely influenced just how much he was willing to discuss with journalists.

However, if JP really wanted to quell the hubbub around his interest in the occult he could have simply fed people with a stock answer until they got sick of the repetition. But he didn't do that; instead deciding to be cryptic and edgy about it which of course created even more interest and speculation. Why? Was this a calculated move to generate curiosity and thus publicity? Was there some sort of an occult-connected intention behind it? We'll explore that later in the book.

Jimmy Page has stated that his interest in the occult really took off when he was fifteen and by his early twenties he was seriously studying Aleister Crowley as well as the various accounts of ancient magicians and, in his words, 'reading about different things that people were supposed to have experienced and seeing whether you could do it yourself'. Magick is about power, being able to affect your lot, your life in a way that allows you to steer the ship versus letting the current take you wherever. People in their twenties, men in particular, often seek that control over the trajectory of their lives and some, like JP, encounter magick.

We do know that Page began collecting Crowley books and memorabilia in the late 1960's which coincides with the time that he founded Led Zeppelin. I think JP and the occult kept bumping into each other until they finally agreed to get together for good. As to why he became fixated on the occult, I think it all comes down to fascination with the unknown.

However, many people become curious about otherworldly things at one point or another in their lives and then it passes or just remains as a mild interest. The occult is like a tractor beam. Some people get close, feel the pull and then back away while others can't resist and allow themselves to be sucked into the void. This is what happened to Jimmy Page. Most of the occult-curious want to see what can be done with this power; how it can benefit them and improve their lives.

As a man in his late teens, did JP intend to use the occult to help his music career? I know I would...hey, anything to give you an extra edge. That's not to suggest that he wouldn't have been enormously talented without the occult. The edge I'm talking about would be along the lines of things that are often left to chance and timing. Things like JP meeting Peter Grant who would become Led Zeppelin's manager and be pivotal in their success. Or let's say the timing of JP meeting Robert Plant who would become the band's vocalist. Then you have John Paul Jones' wife insisting that he reply to a want add for a bassist, etc. What if she didn't push him?

It's those types of things, as well as innumerable other elements of chance, which can be nudged along by occult forces. Some may find this concept far-fetched but there are many that intuitively know these things happen on a daily basis despite the fact that they cannot be proven. Think about it- can anything really be proven? I think proof comes from within; from direct experience and intuition. As a society, we are far too conditioned to only accept proof from bar graphs and men in lab coats. What a boring way to live!

Further down the line, did talismanic magick, as Page had publicly said he used, bring luck with record sales and worldwide fame? Led Zeppelin caught lightning in a bottle, in a very special way. Did they have an edge? If they did, it ultimately proved to be a sharp one.

JP's intentions likely changed as his interest in the occult grew and he saw firsthand what could actually be done. As previously mentioned, my own interest in the occult is why I wrote this book and back when I was deeply into it on an active level, I was always compelled to take things further when I got results.

I think JP was simply having fun, playing with ritual and energy to see what happened and then kept experimenting and using what he had at his disposal. Most people don't have the potent energy of crowds; the focus of thousands of people on them which can be harnessed and directed. Another big component of magick ritual is sexual energy. JP had access to this as well through the endless numbers of groupies offering themselves up to him. More on that later.

Studying the occult is one thing; many people research magick without actually practicing it. I'll bet that the ones who research but do not cross the threshold into practice do so because of fear and/or the idea that magick could not possibly work. However, anyone that spends time reading up on this stuff does wonder what would happen if they actually performed a ritual; even a small quick one. Wouldn't you be tempted? Exactly! But the possibility of opening up Pandora's Box and unleashing something that you couldn't easily get rid of is an understandable deterrent. However, as they say about the cat, curiosity gets the best of us. With youth comes the feeling of invincibility; which gives birth to risks not fully comprehended.

Even though Jimmy Page has been elusive when it comes to discussing his occult studies, he has gone so far as to state during an interview when asked about this- 'I was living it. That's all there is to it. It was my life - that fusion of magick and music.' When asked about his use of sigils (magical seals or marks- we'll get to that later) on the Led Zeppelin IV album as well as on his stage clothing he said 'You mean Talismanic Magick? Yes, I knew what I was doing. There's no point in saying more about it because the more you discuss it the more eccentric you appear to be.'

He closed discussion on the topic with the following statement- 'I'll leave this subject by saying the four musical elements of Led Zeppelin (the members) making a fifth (the music) is magick unto itself. It's the alchemical process.' Another one of Page's comments on magick and Crowley is as follows: 'Magic is very important if people can go through it. I think Aleister Crowley is completely relevant today. We are still seeking for truth—the search goes on.'

Well, there you go. Since we know that Page has actually practiced magick, where did he get his ideas on style of practice and ritual goals? Where did he look for inspiration and direction? Aleister Crowley. And what were the cornerstones of Crowley's magickal practice? Well then, it seems that copious amounts of drugs and sex figured significantly into Crowley's rituals and of course JP had access to endless supplies of both drugs and groupies. Like a mad scientist, he had everything he needed to conduct his experiments after concerts during the wee hours in hotel room laboratories with willing assistants. Where do I sign up?

Aleister Crowley's labeling as 'the wickedest man in the world' was partly due to his recognition of sexual energy as being the most powerful force in the universe. Ok, then there was the demon conjuring and ritualistic sex he had with innumerable men and women. However, his salacious reputation was more of a reflection of the sexual attitudes of late and post-Victorian England.

Sex and self-liberation was a cornerstone to his teachings and of course quite appealing during the 60's and 70's. He knew that sexual energy was a key ingredient to conducting effective occult rituals and saw it as a spiritual rocket fuel of sorts. The Sergeant Pepper album cover appearance that we talked about earlier definitely spurred interest in Crowley among the sexually adventurous youth of the time.

But who exactly was this madman that has influenced and fascinated generations of spiritual seekers and who Jimmy Page once described as a 'misunderstood genius of the 20th century'?

Edward Alexander Crowley was born in Leamington England in 1875. His family were Plymouth Brethren, an evangelical Christian movement that can be traced back to Dublin, Ireland in the 1820's and originates from Anglicanism. Crowley was the son of a wealthy brewing family and was very bright and otherwise normal (whatever that really means) until his beloved father died of cancer when he was just eleven. Didn't we mention earlier that Jimmy Page's first exposure to Crowley was also when he was eleven? They both experienced turning points in their lives at that age.

After his father's death young Aleister became progressively more rebellious. He rejected his parents' religion and turned vehemently anti-Christian. It didn't help that Aleister was not very fond of his strict, domineering mother. Needless to say, the death of a parent at such a critical juncture in development always affects children in profound ways and support or lack thereof following such a tragedy can make all the difference.

In Crowley's case this difference tipped the scales towards animal torture which got him expelled from school and led to home education. Ok; the animal torture thing is a bit of a red flag. Crowley's home-school tutor was a former missionary who taught Aleister about billiards and gambling. Those dodgy missionaries!

Crowley's rebellious streak continued unabated and was marked by sexual promiscuity, continued anti-Christian behavior and all manner of pranks. While a student at

Cambridge his mother died and left him roughly the equivalent of five million dollars in today's money. He left school without finishing his degree, moved to a flat in London and began experimenting with the occult.

During this time he was initiated into the Hermetic Order of the Golden Dawn. Founded by Freemasons, the Golden Dawn is a magical order devoted to the study and practice of the occult, metaphysics and paranormal. A significant portion of the Golden Dawn's practice is based upon the rites of King Solomon which goes back to the 10th century BC. Solomon was the author of one of the most famous grimoires (grammars of magic) known as The Key of Solomon which is based on the biblical story of Angels falling from Heaven. It's a collection of spells and incantations passed down through the centuries which contains detailed instructions on how to cast magic circles and call upon spirits to do various things with their supernatural abilities.

Another of Solomon's grimoires is known as The Lesser Key of Solomon or 'Goetia' which is said to mean howling; some others say it means sorcery. In any event, this dangerous book provides incantations for evoking 72 principal demons and describes them in great detail. I say it's dangerous because I messed with it back in my early 20's and know it works. Part of the reason I wrote this book is because Jimmy Page was particularly interested in the same grimoire and went so far as to publish a new addition of Goetia which had been translated by Crowley and magical cohort S.L. MacGregor Mathers. JP did this through the bookstore he opened in London in 1973 called the Equinox; named after one of Crowley's publications.

Who can really know what JP's motivations were in reprinting a potentially harmful (depending on who is using it) demon conjuring recipe book but I think it's quite telling in two ways. Nobody opens a bookstore like this unless they are very seriously into the occult and to specifically reprint such an ominous spell book is indicative that Jimmy Page most definitely played on the dark side. Did JP practice magick from Goetia? Once again, unless you were there it's impossible to know for sure but why would he have put the effort into reprinting it? It's a safe bet to say that JP, like so many aspiring magicians and occult 'researchers' was curious to see whether or not this demonic recipe book could actually work.

So, after receiving his inheritance Crowley set up camp in London and dove into the highly fascinating world of the occult. He began experimentation using what he'd learned from those around him as well as intense study of Tarot and comparative religion. He then added a twist of drugs and sex and then more drugs and sex...and then some sex and drugs...you get the picture. Sounds like fun to me! That's a big part of why Crowley got such a bad reputation among the prudes back then and he reveled in it and fueled the fire whenever he could.

Like Crowley, Jimmy Page also studied the Tarot and comparative religion. Also like Mr. Crowley, JP enjoyed living a life of groupies and oodles of drugs. The difference here is that while just about all other rock stars were haphazardly engaging in this hedonistic lifestyle, JP had all of the markings of a mad scientist. He was a dedicated student of the occult and had the means to put all of that knowledge into practice.

Did you know that Page has a massive collection of Crowley artifacts such as books, manuscripts, robes and various other objects related to magickal practice? As previously mentioned, Page has also stated on various occasions that he uses Crowley's 'system' and that there's no point in using a system unless it works. Statements like that mean you practice magick, not just read about it.

Unfortunately, most of the general public thinks that any magical practice is Satanic or evil which is why JP has done his best to avoid elaborating on the subject. However, when you're stoned, hyped up on coke and/or excited about this really cool thing you've discovered you do let stuff slip which is why we see little tidbits of JP in interviews corroborating what many have suspected throughout the years. But once the subject is broached he usually answers vaguely and then clams up and gets irritated.

If you do some research you'll find that people close to JP during the 70's have formed a united front stating that he was certainly fascinated with Crowley and the occult but it was all about study and knowledge. They firmly state that JP didn't practice black magic and didn't sell his soul to the Devil, etc. Well yes, I do believe that part as the whole term black magic is so very subjective. Life isn't as black and white as some people would like it to be. However, there's no way around it- Jimmy Page has/does practice magick and I say what's the big deal? Magick takes many forms and happens in daily life a lot more than you'd think.

There is another crucial reason why JP avoids discussing his occult and metaphysical interests. Just as he learned back in the touring days that collective mental focus can be harnessed and directed to achieve a specific outcome, it can also tinker with energetic structures already in place. I'm talking about the effect that a lot of people focusing on him in relation to a particular subject can have.

Famous people receive the vibrational adoration of so many fans that they can feel the effects of this energy whether conscious of it or not. Media coverage of JP's occult interest gets people vibrating or thinking about him in relation to the subject and might very well affect the protective energy he keeps around him or activate dormant energy from a long time ago. One article or interview about JP and the occult could get enough minds focusing on it that 'sleeping' entities flock to him or old negative energy is reconstituted. Yes, this is pretty esoteric stuff but is stock standard in occult circles and if JP were reading this he'd definitely understand what I'm talking about.

So where do Jimmy Page and Aleister Crowley intersect? The trajectories of these two spiritual searchers collide in Inverness, Scotland at a house notorious for otherworldly phenomena. We'll discuss the third main character in this story next. I'm of the opinion that the haunted Boleskine House itself made this fateful introduction (albeit on different timelines).

2 Houses of the Unholy

Aleister Crowley bought Boleskine House in 1899 with the express purpose of performing an elaborate magickal ritual there. Part of this ceremony involved summoning demonic entities and binding them with the goal of removing their negative influences from the magician's life. This sounds sketchy already because, regardless of what any magician tells you, demons cannot be controlled. The ritual and its aftermath is where much of the present-day Boleskine legend comes from. However, this is precisely what made Boleskine House so appealing to Jimmy Page. If you've got the cash and are that much into Crowley, how could you not want such an intriguing piece of property?

Jimmy Page became the owner of Boleskine House in 1970 just as Zeppelin was beginning to enjoy major success. Previous to that we know he had been gathering Crowley artifacts such as old manuscripts, bits and pieces of clothing such as robes and basically anything else he could get his hands on. To be in possession of such a significant piece of Crowley memorabilia was a major score for JP and is indicative of just how passionate and committed he was to the man himself and the occult in general.

However, Boleskine House existed long before the Crowley / Page connection. Legend has it that the house was built on the site of a 10th century Scottish kirk or church which had burned down killing the entire congregation trapped inside. Located 21 miles south of Inverness, halfway between the villages of Foyers and Inverfaragaig, the one story manor was built in the 1760's by Colonel Archibald Fraser as a hunting lodge and expanded several times by the family until 1830. Archibald was related to Lieutenant General Simon Fraser, Lord Lovat.

The house was built on land acquired from the church on a site specifically chosen to annoy Lord Lovat whose estate surrounded the property. Why did Colonel Fraser want to annoy his kinsman? During the Jacobite rebellion of 1745 Lord Lovat had sided with the English; not the best decision to make in Scotland. As you can see, there was already bad blood there which breeds more of the same. As far as the layout goes there were four bedrooms, a kitchen, living room, drawing room and library. Ok, let's go back to the beginning; even before the current structure was there. In many ways this story begins and ends with fire.

Across from Boleskine House, just over the road, is the Fraser clan graveyard. Before the graveyard was there a medieval church stood on the site which had a reputation for strange activity. The only building that remains is a small mort-house which is where the coffined body would remain under guard until it was of no use to the grave robbers prevalent in those days. One legend suggests that there is a tunnel linking Boleskine House to the graveyard. Given that the whole area is former church property and various houses of worship had stood there over the years it sounds fairly reasonable that there might be a leftover tunnel built for practical reasons; now the source of ominous legend.

The burning congregation story is one of the most well-known but another, less common story was uncovered by a schoolteacher doing research on a project for the locality in the 1980's. Since she had actually visited Boleskine House some years earlier as a dinner party guest of Malcolm Dent (JP's old school friend installed as caretaker, who will be discussed shortly) coming across the history of Boleskine graveyard was of considerable interest to her.

The account she found was compiled from the parish archives. In the 2nd half of the 17th century, Minister Thomas Houston (whose stone is still in the graveyard) was roused from his home when a local dark wizard had supposedly raised the bodies of the dead. Minister Houston, doing what ministers do, had to lay the bodies back to rest. It's a creepy story for sure but yes; highly questionable. As Ripley says, you can believe it or not. However, these tales are indicative of the fact that Boleskine House's ominous reputation was not created but certainly enhanced by its future owners. Aleister Crowley's activities there likely took a preexisting rip in the dimensional fabric around the area and tore it wide open.

As a young man, Crowley's fascination with alchemy led him to be acquainted with the leader of the Hermetic Society of the Golden

Dawn. As previously mentioned, the Golden Dawn was a prominent 20th century magical order in Great Britain which significantly influenced Western occult beliefs during that time period. Crowley was quickly initiated into the society by Samuel Lidell MacGregor Mathers. Due to his inheritance, Crowley had the time and resources to focus 100% on his goal of magical enlightenment. This journey led him to Loch Ness in search of the perfect place to perform a ritual that was supposed to put him in contact with his holy guardian angel, or 'higher self'. As mentioned earlier, this ritual would also require summoning demonic forces. What Crowley didn't know at the time was that it would all result in a monumental occult disaster.

As required for the ceremony, Boleskine House was secluded and had a door opening to the North. For those not up on magick, the direction you face when conducting rituals is crucial. Crowley made a few notable modifications. He built a terrace adorned with fine river sand which would allow the footprints of spirits to be seen thus confirming that the ritual was going according to plan.

Crowley considered Boleskine House to be a focal point for mystical energy which made it an ideal place for occult rituals and amplified his belief (which is extremely important in magick) that the operation would work. This particular ceremony was supposed to last a whopping six months. I'm not going to get into the origin of the ritual but will take a moment to give you my take on these recipes from ancient spell books.

Summoning demons and binding them to find your higher self? I know it sounds illogical but supposedly there is a reason for getting evil spirits involved. However; I feel that many of the ancient ceremonies were written by possessed magicians. So actually the spirits themselves prescribed these rituals so as to open the gateways (via the possessed magician) and allow all manner of demonic entities into the physical realm. But magick is all about power and ego so many magicians will disagree with me, thinking that they cannot be controlled by demons; but oh well.

Ok; back to Crowley and his elaborate ceremony. He began the ritual and sure enough it started to work; depending on your definition of work I suppose. You see, he had to summon the demons before he could subdue them. Odd things began to happen. Crowley's lodge keeper, a reformed alcoholic for twenty years, had gone on a three-day bender and tried to kill his wife and children. The lodge keeper was replaced by one of AC's old Cambridge acquaintances but it was said that he was freaked out by the environment too.

Then there's the story of a local butcher accidentally cutting off his hand (or some fingers depending on the source) after reading Crowley's meat order from a scrap of paper that had a spell hastily written on the back. There's more but you get the picture. When you summon demons it's going to affect your environment and the behavior of the people around you. I've lived through this and can tell you it's fascinating but obviously the energy is toxic.

The ritual was interrupted as Crowley was urgently summoned to Paris by a friend. It seems that the head of the Golden Dawn, MacGregor Mathers, was under political pressure from other members of the order and needed Crowley's help. When Crowley finally returned to Boleskine House the place was an energetic mess. He could not banish the dark energies that had entrenched themselves while he was gone. He described physical phenomena that, in his words, was hard to account for. Things like (visual) darkness in the sunniest rooms on the brightest days which could only be remedied with artificial light.

He also described the lodge and terrace being peopled with shadowy figures 'as if the faculty of vision suffered some interference; as if the objects of vision were not properly objects at all.' He further described the figures 'as if they belonged to an order of matter which affected the sight without informing it.' I experienced this exact same optical phenomenon when experimenting with the Goetia in my early twenties. I'd describe it like seeing a large sheet of Saran wrap moving past, just out of the corner of your eye. Something is definitely there and leaves a visual wake of sorts yet it's transparent and disappears as soon as you look directly at it.

Crowley spent little more time in the house as it was too far gone. The demons had taken over and things were way out of balance. Did the ritual actually fail or was it exactly as the demons had intended? Either way, Crowley sold the troublesome property and was off to New York and then Egypt where he was supposedly successful in contacting his guardian Angel. Personally, I think he was under the control of multiple entities that used him as an organic portal to the 3rd dimension. He was in essence a walking demon. Oh well, these things happen...a lot more than you'd think.

Boleskine House changed hands several times over the following years with subsequent owners all experiencing bad luck. For example,

British film star George Sanders wanted to build a pig farm on the property but the venture was a disaster. His partner was sent to jail and all of the animals starved to death. This reminds me of the Amityville Horror film were a pig was used as a representation of the demonic vibration. The animals starving to death would feed the entities on the property with a good meal of trauma energy. These lower astral spirits absorb negative emotions such as pain and try to impulse the physical beings present to create more of it through depression and violent behavior towards themselves and others.

Another owner, a retired Army officer, committed suicide in Crowley's old bedroom in 1960. The officer's former housekeeper shared her experience. Upon arrival, she found the family dog gnawing on a small bone. She picked up the bone, thinking it was stolen from the dinner table or something, and threw it aside. She went to find the army officer and saw him dead in the bedroom with his head blown off. The detectives later told her the bone was from his skull!

All sorts of odd and macabre things supposedly happened over the years and the legend of Boleskine House grew and grew. Needless to say, the locals avoided it like the plague…and still do.

Jimmy Page bought Boleskine House in 1970, just as Led Zeppelin was making its meteoric ascent in the rock world. At that time the property was in considerable disrepair. JP said he hadn't originally intended to buy it but that it was such a fascinating place and 'it just seems to have this thing'. Yes; that thing Page refers to is the astral presences; the lingering entities which he obviously resonated with. I'm not passing any judgment as I have the same 'issue'.

He had the property renovated and installed, as previously mentioned, old school friend Malcolm Dent to run the place while he was off travelling the world touring or otherwise based out of his London home. The official line is that JP spent very little time at Boleskine House. This particular 'fact' is repeated very consistently whenever JP's occult interest is brought up. How is the total length of time he spent there relevant? Does it somehow negate his interest in magick or distance him from Aleister Crowley? Don't lots of rich people own holiday homes out in the country and visit them sporadically?

All we know is that JP held lavish parties there from time-to-time. What happened during those parties? However, it's obvious that JP spent some quality alone time at Boleskine

House as evidenced by this quote. 'You see; people are not used to total quiet and that's what it is there. All I'm saying is that it's a really interesting house and a perfect place to go when one starts getting wound up by the clock. I bought it to go up and write in.'

Whether or not he wasn't there often is not so much a question as why he owned it for twenty two years. Sure, he's incredibly wealthy and why not have such a historic home if you can afford the upkeep. However, I suspect part of the reason he retained the property so long had to do with using it as a generator of sorts, an occult power station.

Ok; you may think this sounds far-fetched but anyone with an understanding of magickal practice knows that objects hold energy and can be tapped into from a distance. While JP was traipsing all over the world he could have very well been using Boleskine House as a source of good fortune and protection. As long as his personal possessions, objects with his energy, were in that house he could be there without being there, so to speak.

Furthermore, each and every movement of Jimmy Page has not been documented over the twenty two years that he owned Boleskine House. Who's to say he didn't shoot over there for a weekend or longer during a tour break or while on hiatus recording a new album. He may very well have spent a lot of time there but we'll never know because JP isn't talking and the people close to him are towing the line.

If he did perform rituals in that house there would be very good reason to hold onto the property even if he really didn't spend much time there. Why? Magick is worked in conjunction with the astral plane and that realm doesn't operate like the physical in terms of time and distance. Intense, focused energy anchors itself to physical objects and locations as there is a correlating astral component or echo to all physical things.

Let's go on the hypothesis that JP performed many rituals at Boleskine House over the years. I'm not suggesting that he practiced black magick although that's quite possible but regardless of the type of ritual the energy will remain in the location it was performed in. So let's say, hypothetically, that JP sells the house a few years later. The new owners could very well disturb that energy and possibly reverse or negate the ritual. They could also undo a protective spell or unleash something contained in the house on an energetic level.

A good way to mitigate the effects of a curse is to create a receptacle of sorts, like a dream catcher, to absorb the malicious energy before it can reach you. This psychic repository of sorts could be broken open buy an unsuspecting person's auric field or perhaps some sort of an intense emotional event in the house and most certainly by potent sexual energy. Owning the house for so long and not living in it would be a good way to keep the toxic energy from spilling out and ricocheting back at you.

Malcolm Dent, JP's old school buddy, lived in Boleskine House with his family for almost twenty two years. He said he was aware that Jimmy had some weird interests but wasn't sure as to the specifics. Dent (who has since passed away) was a rational yet open-minded type. He said he moved in a skeptic yet certainly couldn't explain a lot of the goings-on at Boleskine House. He also conveyed his awareness of the fact that the people of the Scottish Highlands are a lot more superstitious than where he is from in England. He knew that Simon Fraser, Lord Lovat, famous for being the last man beheaded in the UK, was supposedly haunting Boleskine House despite the fact that he was executed before the house was built by his kinsman. Dent said that doors would be slamming all night, rugs were inexplicably found piled up and doors would spring open even during the day.

Demonstrating his casual attitude and humor towards such happenings he said that it was just 'Aleister doing his thing'. He also said that he had regular visits from Crowley followers and other assorted occult lunatics. Jimmy Page sold Boleskine House in 1992 to hotelier Ronald MacGillivray who renovated the property turning it into a luxury residence. The MacGillivrays ultimately sold the house in 2002 and claimed that they did not experience anything unusual. Do you believe them? We will pick up the trail with Boleskine House's fate at the end of the book.

This chapter is titled Houses of the Unholy for a reason. There is another of Aleister Crowley's homes that Jimmy Page considered buying after an alleged visit in 1975. Located in Cefalu, Sicily the Abbey of Thelema was founded by Crowley in 1920. It was intended to be a magickal school and commune of sorts where students could manifest their true will according to Crowley's famous doctrine, Do What Thou Wilt. Jimmy Page was quite fond of the phrase and it basically means do what you were intended to do; find your destiny in life and be happy. It does not mean, as it may initially seem due to the wording, do anything you want regardless of the consequences or how it affects others.

At the Abbey of Thelema inhabitants followed not laws of the spirit but rather desires of the flesh. It eventually devolved into a house of horrors that resulted in the death of twenty three year old Oxford undergraduate Frederick Charles Loveday. Rumors of Satanic worship, sex rituals involving animals (just dreadful) and drug abuse were spread after Loveday's wife, Betty May, gave an interview to the tabloid paper The Sunday Express after returning to London following her husband's death. This created such a scandal that the Italian government finally got involved and demanded that Crowley leave the country in 1923. After all, roughly eighty eight percent of Italy's population is Roman Catholic and this was just too much for them. Who knows what kind of debauchery really occurred at the Abbey of Thelema but reputation has a habit of becoming reality.

Many Crowley fans and researchers have visited this commune of horrors over the years and there is quite a bit about it on the internet. The place looks appropriately creepy and is most certainly haunted. Jimmy Page never actually owned the Abbey of Thelema but he was said to have visited during a fateful trip to Rhodes Greece where Robert Plant got into a very bad car crash. This accident would ultimately become a jump-point of sorts for the Zeppelin Curse.

As the tale goes; Jimmy broke off from the vacation festivities in Rhodes to visit Crowley's Abbey which is precisely when the accident occurred. I cannot definitively confirm this and even the best research is questionable but if it is true then Page was spared injury and possibly death. Was there something occultic afoot here? Possibly, as magick has a funny way of giving and taking with (seemingly) no rhyme or reason. So just how deeply was Led Zeppelin into the occult? Let's have a look...you be the judge.

3 Occult Connections

Among the biggest smoking guns regarding Zeppelin's occult involvement, which is really Jimmy Page's occult involvement, would be their third and fourth albums. The reason I say JP's occult involvement is because up until the tragedy of 1977 (which will be elaborated on later) JP was completely in charge creatively. The others guys were mainly along for the ride and although their input was solicited and appreciated, JP always had the final say which definitely included the occultic references.

Before we get into the specifics I'd like to consider what his drivers might have been.

We're going to have to speculate as of course he wouldn't tell us and even if he did allude to the reasons they'd be laced with cryptic references and would take us down multiple paths leading to nowhere. Such is the nature of the occult. Hidden knowledge is always protected and only the most determined will be able to penetrate this veil. Quite often these fail-safe's are in place to keep the curious from unleashing psychic chaos which they might not be able to cope with.

Why did JP make his occult interest so obvious with these particular albums? It's almost like he was coming out, so to speak. Well, let's just say that the answer is quite simple. He was playing with magick and trying to see just what could be done. He wanted to find out what tangible effects could be discerned from the methods he was applying. He wanted the albums to be successful of course and what better way to give them an extra edge than to inflect them with occult symbolism and energy. Why couldn't he just do something secretly? Why did he make it so obvious? He needed the collective energy, the collective focus, of many minds which would significantly amplify the intended results.

On their third album; known as Led Zeppelin III, the outtro groove had occultic phrases written into the vinyl. This area is located between the end of the last song and the paper label. Ordinarily you'd find matrix numbers from the pressing plant on the outro groove but instead on Zeppelin III was 'So Mote it Be' on one side and 'Do What Thou Wilt' on the other. Whoa; pretty overt, right? Nothing to be speculated on or read into; it's definitely occultic. The phrases are right there, plain as day. So Mote it Be is a stock standard magickal phrase used across the board in many traditions. It basically means 'And so it shall be' and is often used to complete a ritual and seal things off. There is plenty online about this phrase; have a look.

The other one, 'Do What Thou Wilt' is the centerpiece of Crowleyan philosophy. We discussed it earlier but once again it basically means find out what you're meant to do in this life and get on with it. Find your destiny and stay true to it. If one is either on the path to finding their destiny or is currently fulfilling it then life will flow and be joyful. Who doesn't want that, right? This is what Jimmy Page liked about it. Too many people lead their lives according to familial and societal programming without looking within and then become depressed and frustrated. Does this sound familiar? It's quite common and the source of so many of life's ills.

Anyway, so you've got these two phrases written into the vinyl of an album that would go on to sell over six million copies (and counting). Now the originals with the aforementioned phrases carved into the outtro groove number less of course and are now collectors' items. However, that's still a lot of centrifugal force generating magickal energy; which was exactly JP's intention.

From a magickal perspective, words do indeed create and when words (written, spoken or sung) repeat they generate force in the nonphysical realms and eventually spill out into the third dimensional reality we live in. The occult readers will see where I'm coming from and the Zeppelin fans that aren't into or don't believe in magick will disagree- fair enough. The idea was that the energy behind those phrases would spin around and around millions of times all over the world and send those words into the ethers; into the invisible yet just as real place we all pick up on whether consciously or not.

Do you think your cell phone is going to have an effect on your brain if it's sitting right next to your head on the bed table while you sleep? Those transmissions are the same as the ones emanating from a spinning record, just on a more subtle (yet just as effective) frequency. Some people's brains will be more sensitive to this than others and there's really no way to measure the effects but trust me, they do have an impact. This was JP's way of sharing with Zeppelin fans something he was really into and passionate about. It also likely amplified the success of that record and the band overall. Regardless of whether or not this can be proven, the monumental success of the album makes one think...

Led Zeppelin IV took things a few steps further. The album cover and spine did not display the name of the band or a title which the record company had serious issues with. However, Page fought to have his way and said the vague, cryptic nature of the cover was to play down the group's name and basically allow each person to have their own adventure with the album instead of spelling everything out. Inside there's an oil painting which depicts a variation on the Hermit tarot card. JP had professed an affinity for the card and its symbolism.

On the inner sleeve and record label there are four different symbols, each representing a member of the band. Most of these symbols were chosen from the Book of Signs; a collection of ancient and magical symbols from across the world. Needless to say, this was all JP's idea and the rest went along with it although they were allowed to choose their own symbols.

Bassist John Paul Jones' is an ancient Celtic symbol with multiple meanings but basically represents trinity. Lead singer Robert Plant's is the feather of truth from the Egyptian Goddess Ma'at. Drummer John Bonham's symbol, three interlocking rings, either symbolizes a drum kit or the family unit. The most obscure is Page's ZoSo; which he claimed to have designed himself and said he would never reveal the meaning of.

Before we get into the ZoSo symbol let's have a look at the sigil approach to this album. A sigil is a sign or image which supposedly has magical power. Technically speaking, a symbol is a character or glyph representing an idea, concept or object while a sigil is a seal, signature or signet. However, although different, the terms sigil and symbol can be used interchangeably. From a magickal perspective, sigils bypass the conscious mind and go directly to the subconscious.

One can make their own sigil or use a preexisting one and 'charge' it with specific, personal intentions. These intentions could be good luck or protection or the sigil could be charged with malicious intent and left around for someone to see or posted to them in the mail, etc. This someone would be the magician's target and depending on their understanding of the occult would be adversely affected by the sigil as its poison would go directly into their unconscious setting off a chain reaction of internal damage. This damage could be exactly as the magician intended or very well manifest differently depending on whether or not the target has taken protective measures.

So for instance, if the attacking magician has intended a car accident and death but the target has protected themselves they may just get a flat tire and pull over to the side of the road; something along those lines. This protection could be conscious or unconscious as some people intuitively know when they are under psychic attack and others are always protecting themselves because they are occultists who regularly engage in magickal tit-for-tat warfare. There are innumerable variables which could indicate protection/shielding.

Preexisting sigils are often used in magickal attacks. For instance, the demonic sigils in the Goetia spell book (which, as referenced earlier, JP had specifically reprinted through his Equinox occult bookstore) could be used to hurt someone. A particular demon whose purpose is, for example, to create illness would somehow be delivered to the target to set off a chain reaction of damage. There are negative and positive uses for sigils but magick is generally about power and eventually (whether consciously or not) a magician is likely going to be led down questionable paths. Let's get back to the ZoSo sigil.

JP chose the preexisting ZoSo sigil for Zeppelin IV and also used it on his performance attire and musical equipment. Although he said he designed it, the symbol's origins go back to at least 1557 which we'll discuss in a moment. However, he may have meant that he designed it in the sense of personalized it which could be interpreted as creating. ZoSo is said to represent the planet Saturn which rules over JP's astrological sun sign, Capricorn. This is likely why he chose it.

By the way, of the two books that JP specifically had reprinted and distributed through his bookstore the other (along with Goetia) was a book on astrology. Jimmy Page said he'd never tell anyone what ZoSo means to him or why he chose it so we'll probably never know for sure.

Despite Jimmy Page's conscious intentions with the use of ZoSo it's almost certain that the sigil magnetized dark energies (demons, evil spirits, whatever you want to call them). Here's the problem with that stuff and believe me I know. Once you start messing with these pictorial representations of energy you become 'tagged' on the astral plane. The astral is generally agreed to be the next frequency or reality beyond the physical. It's the repository of our thoughts, desires and emotions. It's also where ghosts, demons and other sentient and non-sentient consciousness exist.

There is a lot of argument in paranormal circles as to what the astral is and contains. However, let's just say that JP's energy signature was most certainly glowing with that 'I'm a believer in the nonphysical and interested in engaging with it' invitation. Once tagged you're open to all sorts of manipulation and it's virtually impossible to decipher what's what. You are basically floating in an ocean and could run into sharks and/or dolphins depending on what you're aligning with.

In regards to ZoSo, JP was most definitely playing with dangerous energies as many, many occult practitioners do. Why? Well, it's pretty exciting to interact with gnarly, paranormal stuff. It's kind of like shark diving. People get a rush out of facing a Great White; risking death and living to tell the tale. What's so dark about ZoSo? I'll explain in a moment.

Since Page was a follower of Crowley I can only surmise that he, like Crowley, rationalized his interaction with demonic energies by thinking that evil is just a label and it's all a matter of perception, etc. How do I know this? Because I thought the same thing regarding my experiments with the Goetia grimoire and other rituals. I thought; there is no good or evil, that's such a simplistic, un-evolved way of looking at things. And to be fair, I get the feeling that JP was just curious and don't think he had any malevolent intentions. I could be wrong about him and wrong about Crowley aligning with darker energies but we'll never know.

The danger in working with certain types of sigils is that vampiric entities, like tapeworms, can work their way into your thought processes and start introducing ideas that in the beginning closely match your own thinking so as not to alarm the host (you). Once you're used to their presence they slowly begin to bend your thought patterns in a decidedly unhealthy manner and slowly but surely you start to change.

I went through it and can spot the signs a mile away. Occultists that vehemently disagree or react aggressively to such concepts are surely under foreign influence themselves and must come to this conclusion in their own time. The ritual magician's weakness is the desire for power and entities have a massive advantage when it comes to infiltrating a human's mind. Once you cross that threshold you'll never be the same; never.

Remember, I'm not saying that Jimmy Page is a Satanist or evil, etc. but he definitely flirted with questionable energies which I cannot judge him for as I did the same. I'm simply making observations based on the information available. Hey, it certainly appears that he had a lot of fun despite the bad luck and upheaval the band experienced from the mid 70's onward.

Before we go further into the ZoSo sigil, this is just a bit of a disclaimer for the occult scholars out there. I'm going to touch upon it in sufficient detail for the purposes of this book. However, there are more connections that could be made and there are other places the sigil can be found which I don't mention. This is a hall of mirrors I don't want to linger in as it doesn't sit well with me so you won't find every detail on ZoSo...but of course there is the internet. Be careful...

As previously mentioned, ZoSo is associated with the planet Saturn which is in turn associated with Satan. Jimmy Page's astrological sign is Capricorn and the symbol for Capricorn is the goat which is associated with the Devil or Satan depending on how one interprets it. Following on with ZoSo's origins, the sigil is also connected to the 12th century alchemist Artephius. Mathematician and occultist Gerolamo Cardano included the ZoSo symbol in a chapter of his 1557 book De Rerum Varietate which discussed the magick of alchemist Artephius. By the way, Cardano's text was placed on the Vatican's list of forbidden books.

The symbol can also be found in reprints of a grimoire from the 1500's known in English as The Red Dragon and the Black Hen as well as a rare 19th century dictionary of symbols called Le Triple Vocabulaire Infernal Manuel du Demonomane. Regardless of where JP found the ZoSo symbol I don't really pick up on any positive connotations with those names, do you? Have a look at the symbol itself on the internet as well as the books it came from. What kind of a vibe do you get? I'm not here to judge but I do encourage using your gut, the only reliable barometer of truth, to get a sense of the energy certain things carry with them. JP was playing with dark stuff here and it may very well have empowered him to a degree but it's always a slippery slope.

Page had the ZoSo sigil on his performance clothing and equipment and since he confirmed his practice of Talismanic Magick one can surmise that he 'charged' it with his own personal intentions. He could have used it for protection and/or as a magnet for the band's success. (Yes, dark energies can help you but it usually comes at a price.) The advantage of being in front of thousands of people on a regular basis is that the talisman's effectiveness would be significantly amplified by the power of the subconscious minds of those watching. You don't have to consciously know what ZoSo means to Jimmy Page to help him fortify this occult magnet/shield.

There are so many powerful variables at play here. The vibration of the music would open up the auric fields of those in attendance and then their own personal attachment to the music would feed energy through to the stage; through to JP. Think about it; they are at a live Zeppelin concert watching their heroes play in person; right in front of them! Each fan's magnetic power is at full wattage while listening to the music and then their eyes see the ZoSo symbol and subconsciously pick up on JP's energy of intention and unknowingly feed it with their juice.

Yes, this is all very esoteric and unprovable but that is magick. Believe me; people wouldn't practice it if it didn't work. This whole Zeppelin thing was a unique experiment in that of course not all magicians had the energetic battery power of thousands at their disposal and few if any musicians had the depth of occult knowledge or will to use it.

Now Jimmy Page said he would never reveal what ZoSo means to him but Robert Plant once mentioned that JP told him but he was high and/or drunk at the time and had forgotten by morning. He said he asked JP about it again but JP clammed up and said he couldn't tell him. As previously discussed, Page is quite offish when it comes to talking about his interest in the occult but he has slipped here and there. In my opinion, this reluctance comes from a mixture of things.

Part of it is a desire to be cryptic thus generating more interest and speculation which then feeds the myth and creates more occult energy/power for increased album sales. Part of him also wants to share with others what he finds so interesting and invigorating but the occult is a subject which usually results in hair-trigger judgment, fear and ultimately a Devil worshipper label with the masses. I can see why this would piss him off and create a hot/cold attitude towards discussing it. Another reason Jimmy Page doesn't reveal too much, as in the case with the ZoSo and Robert Plant story above, is the energy behind the subject and the entities attached to it.

For JP to tell people what ZoSo means to him could very well agitate the nonphysical beings associated with it and potentially result in a punishment or backlash of sorts. With the occult you just never know what's going on in the background and directing too much focus (by publicly talking about it) on a particular sigil could break energy locks or upset a delicate balance related to a spell or magickal working. It's also quite possible that Plant remembered what JP told him that night and backtracked mid-sentence when he realized what it could mean to reveal this information. People very often start a sentence or train of thought with a particular intent only to switch gears and cover things up mid-stream. We want to share things as that's human nature but another voice comes in and tells us to be careful.

The last thing I'll say about ZoSo is that it's allegedly connected to a demon called ZoZo and the Ouija board. I'll let you do your own research on this one. There's enough out there to draw parallels between ZoSo and some decidedly creepy stuff so even if JP had positive intentions, the slipstream that occult correlations can create may have overrode that.

Let's have a look at occult symbolism in Zeppelin's lyrics as well. Many of you probably know that Stairway to Heaven is the most highly requested radio song of all time. Those famous first chords are among the most identifiable in rock history. Some eight minutes long, it plays out as a mystical quest of sorts with elements of paganism and mythology all mixed in to create an experience that is still being had daily on classic rock stations all over the planet. The song's theme has been explained by some as a search for meaning in a world of ambiguity which is the ideal playground for deeply accessing the subconscious.

Stairway has been described as not just a song but a spell. I'd say that's dead-on for a number of reasons. The spells that are cast during occult rituals gain power through belief, emotion and repetition as these important elements accumulate energy; very much like the buildup to sexual climax. Sound has supreme power in magick as the vibrations that sounds create are a bridge between the 3rd and 4th dimensions. This is why so many occult traditions utilize bells, drums and song when communicating with the invisible beings they seek assistance from. We'll go into rock concerts as ritual in the next chapter but the keys here are sound and repetition which have perpetuated the endless spell that Stairway to Heaven has become.

Jimmy Page and Robert Plant have publicly alluded to a number of their songs being 'channeled'. In the case of Stairway to Heaven they have undeniably stated it. Plant said that the lyrics were written (by his hand) while he was unaware of what was happening to him. This is commonly known as automatic writing or channeling in spiritualist and occult circles. Basically, you relax and open yourself up with pen in hand and paper in front of you. This happens to some people without them consciously asking for it and others intentionally will it upon themselves.

Ideally you should clear your space or do a purification of some sort before opening yourself up to the highly unreliable and suspect spirit world. This purification can take many forms and could involve verbally banishing negative entities or creating a magick circle, etc. The list could go on and on and although there is no guarantee that purifications work it's at least worth a shot. However, in the other category you have the folks that consciously open themselves up and don't do a purification or those that aren't really aware of what is happening and of course no protective action is taken.

There are many that have practiced different types of channeling techniques for years and claim no adverse effects. This could very well be true but as I mentioned earlier, the spirit world cannot be scientifically measured nor trusted in any way, shape or form. I said scientifically but only in the 3rd dimensional sense. I still believe magick is a science but unfortunately it will never fit into an acceptable, measurable context recognized by the masses. But who cares, right? Once you know this stuff is real through direct experience, other people's validation is irrelevant.

Work on Stairway to Heaven supposedly began in a 250 year old Welsh cottage called Bron-yr-Aur. As the story goes, Plant and Page were by the fire one night when Plant jotted down the first words to the song. He later claimed that the lyrics came to him, as if written automatically. He remembered being in a very bad mood and was just sitting there with paper and pencil in hand and all of a sudden he was writing out the words to Stairway to Heaven. He said that he almost jumped out of his seat.

However, Jimmy Page told a different story under oath during a 2016 plagiarism trial over the song. He stated that he wrote the music on his own and first played it for the rest of the band at an old stone castle in England called Headley Grange. Zeppelin fans will likely know of this place as it was used as a recording and rehearsal venue by many famous bands in the 60's and 70's. Parts of four different Zeppelin albums were composed and/or recorded at Headley Grange so it's obviously a significant location for the band. Plant also confirmed this version of the story under oath. So what's the truth? The automatic writing story is pretty creepy but was it nonsense?

Now to be fair, this happens to some degree quite often and I'll bet many artists of all types will agree that some form of communion with the spirit world or another part of their consciousness (who can say which is which) occurs when they get into the 'zone' or tap into their inspiration to create art. However, this is Led Zeppelin and the occult will always be inextricably linked to them.

A curious detail is that Plant said he was in a very bad mood and even emphasized this when telling the story as if it was such a foul mood that it left an indelible impression. This could be due to the fact that there were dark entities present and he picked up on it. Uniquely bad moods are a classic indicator of spirit presence. Hey, you never know. Call it a stretch but it's rather interesting that these details and sequence of events are there.

Whether or not Plant sharing the automatic writing story publicly was just him having fun and stoking the Zeppelin lore is anyone's guess but that angle has to be considered as well. Flirting with the occult can give a band's image an edge (Ozzy Osbourne comes to mind) that will translate into more success but there often comes a point where it gets too close for comfort. Plant eventually had enough of the mystical stuff and tried to wash his hands of it after the Zeppelin began to plummet and the bad luck crept in.

This also happened to the Rolling Stones' Mick Jagger who distanced himself from the occult image he cultivated following a string of ill fortune and deaths as well. We'll elaborate on that a bit later as a Stones connection factors into my conclusion as to who or what might be responsible for the Led Zeppelin Curse.

I'm sure some of you have heard about the supposed backmasked Satanic messages in Stairway to Heaven's lyrics. Backmasking is a recording technique in which a message or sound is recorded backward onto a track that is meant to be played forward. It can be traced all the way back to Thomas Edison who invented the phonograph in 1877. Edison thought that music in reverse sounded very interesting and made note of it.

In the 1950's creative musicians picked up on this and began working it into their tunes by running reel-to-reel tape recorders backwards. A decade later the Beatles experimented with backmasking and a couple of their songs are cited among the most famous examples of this technique. What I find interesting here is that (as previously mentioned) Aleister Crowley made an appearance on the album cover of Sergeant Pepper and the Satanic connection to backmasking can be traced back to one of Crowley's books.

It seems that all roads lead back to Uncle Aleister when it comes to this stuff. In the book Crowley recommends that those interested in Black Magick would do well to learn how to think and speak backwards. Stairway to Heaven allegedly has an ominous message hidden in the following passage:

'If there's a bustle in your hedgerow, don't be alarmed now, it's just a spring clean for the May Queen.

Yes there are two paths you can go by, but in the long run, there's still time to change the road you're on.'

When played in reverse this is what can supposedly be heard by some…

'Oh here's to my sweet Satan. The one whose little path would make me sad, whose power is Satan. He will give those with him 666.

There was a tool shed where he made us suffer, sad Satan.'

Pretty creepy, huh? I don't know about you but it makes me feel yuk. We all interpret things through our own lenses of perception but I'll tell you what I see here. The May Queen references May Day, May 1st which has Pagan origins and is considered a very powerful holiday by several different religious and quasi-religious groups. May 1st has even been co-opted by the Illuminati as a high ritual day. We're not going down the path of conspiracies but suffice to say that Satanic rituals are practiced by the Illuminati and the first day of May is a biggie for them. There is quite a bit online regarding the Illuminati's alleged connection to the music industry.

Ok; back to the Stairway lyrics interpretation. The whole two paths you can go by phrase refers to the two paths in magick. The left path is considered dark and the right path is considered light. The whole concept of light and dark is too simplistic and utterly ridiculous to me; but anyway. So the suggestion that there are two paths means that there's a choice and also that even if you chose one you can switch. This makes the idea of going down the dark path (which is usually more interesting to rock fans) seem quite safe and reversible which is definitely not the case as it's a slippery slope once you engage with that type of energy. The road you're on could very well stand in for the Highway to Hell.

Now the reversed message interpretation. Just calling Satan sweet is indicative of a relationship of some sort. It's a very creepy expression when referring to that type of energy. Next we have road and path again so the Highway to Hell but calling it little is a way of making it creepier and more intrusive as it sounds almost harmless when it certainly isn't. Giving those with him 666 is giving them the mark of the Beast. The whole tool shed suffering thing made me think of child abuse which just really puts this passage into the utterly vile category. I feel like I need a shower after reading that.

Now let's talk about the effect it would have on the subconscious minds of the millions of people listening to the song over and over. That decidedly icky vibe traveling directly through the backdoor of your mind will affect thoughts and emotions as well as drive behavior. The fact that this insidious backmasking has been revealed makes it no less powerful. On the contrary, it becomes more effective because you think since it's been called out it loses its power but that is not the case. Much like an overt compliment that you suspect has been given for manipulative purposes, being aware of backmasking doesn't negate its power over the subconscious. So when did all of this come to the public's attention?

Back in 1981 a Michigan minister named Michael Mills announced on Christian radio that Stairway to Heaven contained backmasked Satanic messages. Bear in mind that this allegation came ten years after the song's release. Was there any wisp of this backmasking before then? Actually; rumors of these covertly placed messages began in 1975 when the Zeppelin began to plummet. Once Robert Plant and his family were involved in a bad car accident while on holiday in Rhodes Greece, talk of the Zeppelin Curse began to circulate by word of mouth. That event was one of the main triggers for other things like the backmasking story.

It makes you wonder how all of this would have tracked in the internet age. Would the story surface only to be squashed by it going viral and then negated online? I suppose that's neither here nor there but perhaps the slow progression of such a mystery and the time it had to percolate might have given it the necessary oxygen to flourish. The exact origin of the backmasking story will never be known but it could very well have been a genius marketing ploy. The band's trailblazing manager, Peter Grant, was a master marketer and knew the power of word of mouth.

Just because I'm approaching this from an occult perspective doesn't mean that I necessarily believe in the hidden messages as they are highly questionable. I've listened and feel that the mind can definitely trick you into hearing things that aren't really there. I think I heard some of those words but because I read up on it ahead of time my interpretation has been tainted. You can find it online; let me know what you think. The bottom line is that this backmasking story is out there and that feeds the myth. It's a piece of the foundation however faulty it might be.

If you find the backmasking connection questionable then the overtly occult lyrics of the song Houses of the Holy might help you change your tune. My take on it is in bold between the verses. It goes into areas beyond the scope of this book but you'll understand where I'm coming from. As always; it's just an interpretation- accept or reject as you see fit.

HOUSES OF THE HOLY (lyrics)

Let me take you to
the movies.
Can I take you to the
show
Let me be yours ever
truly.
Can I make your
garden grow

The movie reference is all about the occultic / Satanic influence on Hollywood. There is significant data, both past and present, that Hollywood is a town drenched in dark energy. Have a look online- you'll see. Remember; these lyrics were fed / channeled (in part) by entities through Page & Plant. Making the garden grow is pure sexual innuendo which is the main delivery mechanism of this Satanic agenda.

From the houses of the holy,
we can watch the white doves go
From the door comes Satan's daughter,
and it only goes to show.
You know.

White doves- strong occult symbolism. From the door- doors of perception / mind altering. Satan's daughter- no explanation needed.

There's an angel on my shoulder,
In my hand a sword of gold

Let me wander in your garden.
And the seeds of love I'll sow.
You know.

Angel on my shoulder has a double meaning as Lucifer was/is (after all) an Angel. Sword of gold refers to Lucifer's sword. Wander your garden and seeds sexual. Sowing... implanting (via sex) demonic energies/mind control into the auric field.

So the world is spinning faster.
Are you dizzy when you're stoned
Let the music be your master.
Will you heed the master's call
Oh... Satan and man.

Spinning- mind altering thus susceptible to control/influence. Let the music take over Satan is your master.

Said there ain't no use in crying.
Cause it will only, only drive you mad
Does it hurt to hear them lying?
Was this the only world you had?
Oh-oh

Don't cry/complain- just accept your fate as Satan's minion. Does it hurt to hear them (Satan/demons) lying to you? They now control your only world. This is like rubbing salt in the wound; laughing at the fact that the listener was complicit in their own degradation/giving away of their power.

So let me take you,
take you to the movie.
Can I take you, baby, to the show.
Why don't you let me be yours ever truly.
Can I make your garden grow

Back to the movie- a way of sealing the deal / closing the loop / finishing the ritual. Give yourself over to me so I can entrance / control you sexually.

You know.

You were aware of this and let it happen.

I spoke a bit about the mind control aspect of this which works hand-in-hand with the demonic realm. If you're interested in looking further into this stuff check out my first book which is (at the time of this writing) under a pen name and referenced in my author bio. It's a bit crazy- not for everyone.

So those were the lyrics; now let's look at the album cover of Houses of the Holy. There's a good chance you've seen this image, even if you're not a Zeppelin fan. It depicts naked, golden-haired children crawling around what is most often described as an apocalyptic landscape. Have a look online and see what you think. I see a pyramid of sorts. A parallel has also been drawn to the 1950's sci-fi movie Village of the Dammed which I can understand given the seemingly hypnotized children.

It has been revealed that the cover was based on Arthur C. Clarke's novel Childhood's End which definitely makes sense given that the book is about children congregating to be taken into space. I see it more as the kids going into the pyramid thus being hypnotized into going off to inner-space; the landscape of the mind. This cover did its job of generating lots of interest and speculation as any good marketing is supposed to do.

The inner sleeve depicts a naked adult holding a child over their head in front of the ruins of a castle. It's definitely indicative of ritual sacrifice and is quite creepy. All of it is creepy; the lyrics, cover and inner sleeve do their job of flirting with the dark side which is very effective in the rock world. The occult themes of the Devil / Piper entrancing the children (cover) and then sacrificing them (inner sleeve) are certainly there although it's left vague enough to allow each individual their own interpretation. The ambiguity makes it even more personalized and thus potent on a subconscious level.

Yet another occultic image from Zeppelin is their record label's logo. The Swansong label uses a riff on the William Rimmer painting 'Evening – The Dawn of Day' which is most often thought to depict the God Apollo (associated with Lucifer) or possibly Icarus or

Daedalus from the ancient fable. Rimmer never specified so we'll never know and it really doesn't matter as the important thing is what Jimmy Page wanted it to represent. I'd wager that he had Lucifer in mind. But the mainstream's first reaction to this is that Lucifer is 'evil'; whatever that really means.

Remember though; Lucifer was the first Angel, God's favorite, the Light Bearer. He/She just happened to question God and became the rebel. Doesn't everyone go through that phase? Funny how societal conditioning works. I suspect JP had this in mind when he chose that image to represent Swansong.

Lucifer is edgy and double meanings abound depending on one's interpretation so once again while it's definitely occult symbolism I don't think there was any evil overtone implied. People that have explored the good/evil conundrum often enjoy pushing the buttons of those narrow-minded black/white people like religious fanatics, etc. That said; even fairly open-minded people have a knee-jerk reaction to the mention of Lucifer. After all, he/she is the villain from antiquity.

The last bit of evidence regarding occult symbolism I'd like to touch upon comes from Zeppelin's concert film The Song Remains the Same. There is what is known as 'the Hermit

Sequence' involving Jimmy Page climbing up the face of a snow-capped mountain. The mountain that was used for the scene was very close to Boleskine House and Aleister Crowley had hiked up it many times while living there back in the early 1900's.

The Hermit refers to a tarot card that JP was particularly fond of. The scene was meant to show JP on a quest for enlightenment by seeking out the Hermit. This Hermit character is usually depicted on the summit of a mountain with the Staff of Wisdom in one hand and the Lantern of Knowledge in the other. The Hermit represents an obstacle or gatekeeper the seeker must overcome to achieve the enlightenment they are after.

At the end of this sequence in Song Remains the Same JP reaches out to touch the Hermit only to find that the Hermit is himself. Pretty cool; check it out online. Nothing evil there and that pretty much sums up JP's general approach to the occult. Unfortunately, it doesn't necessarily work that way when you occasionally wade into the deep, dark water as Zeppelin did from time to time. There may not have been any malicious intent but just interacting with dark entities, even out of pure curiosity, puts you on an irreversible trajectory that can last lifetimes. I'm not kidding.

For example, Jimmy Page's purchase of Boleskine House as a Crowley acquisition/artifact most definitely facilitated spirit attachment due to the residual demonic forces there. The Houses of the Holy lyrics that we just discussed is another example of playing with fire. Just because you never summoned demons to try and hurt or kill someone does not mean that you can intentionally be in their environment without an extremely high level of risk.

Lot's of occult symbolism there, right? We could go on and on but I think we've explored that enough. Let's have a look at rituals next!

4 Concert as Ritual

As you know, rock concerts are exciting, frenetic, and some would even say orgiastic events. The scientific community is well aware of the potential consciousness altering effects that music can have. However, the kind of music and more specifically the harmonics involved will have a significant impact on the type of experience the listener has. Everything comes down to vibration and music creates ripples that call out to the more subtle realities around us. The density of the musical vibration will correlate with the quality of the dimension the music taps into.

Like attracts like and the type of music being played at a concert will connect to the worlds and the entities contained therein which match that frequency. So basically, rock concerts attract flesh and blood human fans as well as nonphysical energies (ghosts, spirits, etc.) that are pulled through the veil which is unlocked by the vibration of the music.

Now I'm not here to pass judgment and say that 'negative' energies flock to rock concerts because such labels are all relative. I'd rather look at it on a horizontal scale and just say that the types of entities attracted to a symphony performance are going to be different than ones brought in by a Led Zeppelin concert. Neither is better or worse; more or less evolved than the other, etc. However, you'll definitely see more overt manifestation or evidence of spirit presences at rock concerts than you would at symphony performances and here's why.

The body is very much an instrument unto itself and we all 'feel' music, don't we? So if you just relax and open up when listening to classical music the vibrations that are 'playing' your body will generally make you feel calm and some would even say spiritually elevated. Now relax, open up and play Led Zeppelin's Immigrant Song. I love that one and the feeling it creates within me is fantastic! I feel adrenalized, on fire, the blood starts to pump.

However, when these particular musical vibrations fill the air and your body, your instrument, starts responding to the beat, two things happen. The music 'sings' out to the other dimensions and attracts the types of beings that resonate with that particular frequency. Then your body responds to the musical vibrations and becomes a gateway. You are now a portal to allow these nonphysical energies to enter into and experience the physical realm. Pretty freaky, huh?

Of course I cannot scientifically prove this concert leading to temporary possession ritual theory but if you do some research you'll see there is significant evidence pointing in that direction. For centuries (and even longer), many cultures have been purposely using music in ritual to invite spirits into the bodies of their priests and priestesses. Jimmy Page has gone on record describing Zeppelin concerts as a form of ritual and he knew very well the amount of energy that could be generated during a live performance and more importantly what could be done with it.

Back in 1975 Jimmy Page was interviewed by famous beat generation writer William Burroughs. The writer attended a

Zeppelin concert and documented his
experience describing the ritualistic nature of the
performance and that leaving the auditorium felt
like getting off a jet plane. If you've ever
attended a rock concert you'll definitely relate to
that. He felt that the Led Zeppelin concert
depended on volume, repetition and drums;
similar to the trance music of Morocco. This
music's origin is magical and is focused on the
evocation and control of spiritual forces. In
Morocco the musicians are also magicians, like
snake charmers, and their music is used to drive
out evil spirits as well as bring good/beneficial
ones in.

Continuing with his analysis, Burroughs
went on to say that a Led Zeppelin concert
would be focused on the creation of energy in
both the performers and the audience but
warned that tapping into this energy could be
dangerous. He further described a rock concert
as nothing more than a ritual where psychic
power is released and transformed; an
interchange of energy between the band and the
audience which circulates and builds throughout
the performance. He likened the musicians to
priests presiding over a mass focused on the
evocation and transmutation of energy.

During this conversation Page and
Burroughs discussed the energy of a crowd and

wondered if the power of collective concentration might create, if directed properly, a sort of experiential stairway to heaven. Please bear in mind that Jimmy Page isn't shy about shutting an interviewer down if he doesn't agree with their line of questioning or beliefs in relation to the subject matter being discussed. Following on with the previous comment about concert energy potentially being destructive, Burroughs noted that when this experiential stairway to heaven becomes possible is the moment of greatest danger. Page, obviously being aware of such dangers, commented that one must be careful with large audiences and compared it to driving a load of nitroglycerin.

This really interesting discussion Page and Burroughs had also covered JP's Boleskine House on Loch Ness during which the guitarist confirmed that it's haunted and that he also believes in the Loch Ness monster. Another topic they touched upon was infrasound. Allegedly developed as a weapon by the French military, infrasound is pitched below the level of human hearing (16 Hertz) which can kill a human being by attacking the organs. Also mentioned was interspecies communication with sonar waves, specifically with dolphins, and the trance music of Morocco.

Although very stream of consciousness (no surprise there with Burroughs) the theme of this particular part of the chat was rhythm, vibration and their effects on the human body. JP added his two cents by stating that music involves riffs which will have a trancelike effect on the listener. He went on to compare riffs with mantras and said the band had been criticized for intentionally creating mind altering riffs that incited violence and provocative behavior.

In many respects the audience is also an instrument; a larger instrument being collectively played by the band. As previously mentioned, ritual by its very nature is all about repetition and Led Zeppelin spent night after night performing the same songs before very captive audiences full of young people brimming with energy. Hearing a band's music on the radio is one thing but a live performance is an experience involving all of the senses.

If you can imagine how you've felt at a concert and then multiply that by a hundred thousand it'll give you an idea of how much energy is generated. Jimmy Page surely played with this energy and his knowledge of magick gave him the tools to harness and direct the immense potential available to him night after night on the road.

But did Jimmy Page practice magick rituals during his performances? He has certainly been accused of attempting to hypnotize countless fans with hidden meanings in lyrics and other methods such as body language and through the symbols that adorned his stage clothing and equipment. JP's violin bow solos have been singled out as blatant evidence of these covert yet overt ceremonies. Yes, the violin bow could certainly be used as a magic wand of sorts.

His use of the violin bow/wand in conjunction with a Theremin is a sight to behold. A Theremin is an electronic instrument in which tone is generated by two high frequency oscillators and the pitch is controlled by the movement of the performer's hand. It creates a delightfully eerie sound; akin to what you might hear in a 1950's sci-fi or horror movie.

Page has definitely performed the 'Four Corners' ritual with his wand and Theremin onstage. Any occultist will tell you this standard ritual is used to cleanse a space and prepare for spell work. It is also used to close ceremonies and is alternatively known as Calling the Corners, Casting the Circle and The Lesser Banishing Ritual. It all depends on the magical tradition you are following but regardless of the many different names and variations of this ritual the goals are the same. Look this up on YouTube: Led Zeppelin – Dazed and Confused (violin bow) NY 1973. Use your gut- he's not going to say into the microphone 'I'm going to do a ritual now' but it's very obvious that he's focusing his energy with the violin bow. I love it- gives me the chills!

But does this constitute proof of purposely conducted onstage occult rituals? Nope; absolutely not and there's no way to definitively show that JP was intentionally trying to control or manipulate the audience. However, any good ritual magician will tell you it's focused energy and intent that make a ceremony effective. Body language and symbols only serve to bolster those all-important mental powers which are the keys to successfully manipulating the physical plane and those residing on it.

Since we're on the topic of concerts and being on the road, there are rumors of JP practicing occult rituals in hotel rooms. I've come across this several times online and yes, it could very well be absolute BS but that's what has circulated and it's not just one mention; there is enough to make you wonder. This segues nicely into our next topic of sex ritual groupie experimentation. However, I think it's important to clarify what we mean by ritual as quite often (whether consciously or not) there are negative connotations attached to the word.

Just because one practices a ritual doesn't make them evil or have malicious intent. A ritual could very well be focused on bringing good things into your life and creating harmony, etc. In fact, that's what all magick is intended to do; use the power of the mind to harness what's available within and without to create anything you want. However, there's often a problem with this. When you willingly try and tap into the invisible worlds, regardless of your intent or how experienced and knowledgeable you might be, you cannot control what shows up.

The nonphysical ocean all around us contains many fascinating and beautiful creatures. Just because you call dolphins doesn't mean that only dolphins will appear. There could be sharks and much like a dorsal fin cutting through the water it's hard to tell at first glance whether there's a dolphin or shark attached to it. So yes; even the most benign ritual can result in a feeding frenzy and bloodbath.

However, this isn't always the case. I can hear some practitioners saying that they've performed rituals all of their life and have had no issues. First this depends on how you define issues and secondly, entity influence can be very hard to identify as the practitioner because you're too close to the situation to see the subtle yet potentially dangerous influences around you. But no; not all magickal ceremony results in negative effects but it does open that door. Ok; let's get back to the groupies.

Rock stars and groupies go together like hot dogs and ketchup, like carrots and dip and like bullets and guns. Aside from fame and fortune, being a rock god brings sex, lots of it! As we've discussed, Jimmy Page was heavily into notorious occultist Aleister Crowley and all that it implies. A huge part of Crowley's magickal philosophy and system involved sex ritual. A rock star travelling the world with continuous access to nubile women willing to do anything and everything to please him creates the perfect occult laboratory. Imagine JP reading about Crowley's sex magick rituals one moment and the next he hears a knock at the hotel room door. It's his road manager with a bevy of babes ready to party. Well there you go...

What is sex ritual? It means many things to many people but I'll give you my brief definition. During the sexual act we as humans are at our most vulnerable but also most powerful. Generating sexual energy all by yourself (you know what I mean) is quite potent but when two (or more) humans combine this energy in a focused manner the results can be amazing. Sex ritual goes back in time as far as the eye can see. Unfortunately, the church came in and screwed, pardon the pun, everything up with their guilt programming and other control mechanisms.

I won't go on and on here (my other books talk about this a lot more) but suffice to say that having sex with the specific purpose of creating or tapping into something can lead to physical manifestation at an extremely accelerated rate. Aleister Crowley experimented heavily with sex ritual and then added drugs to the mix to amplify the results. He called his sex ritual partners Scarlet Women.

If you start researching Crowley the term Scarlet Woman will sure enough arise. The dictionary defines a Scarlet Woman as a sinful, immoral, promiscuous woman; especially a prostitute or woman that commits adultery. The term can be found in the bible and also in Crowley's religion, Thelema, where the Scarlet Woman is an oracle of sorts. The old magician spent a great deal of time looking for (and copulating with) his various appointed sacred prostitutes. These women were sex magick partners meant to enhance rituals and bring through energy and results that Crowley could not easily produce by himself.

He had multiple Scarlet Women during his heyday and paradoxically treated them in both demeaning and respectful ways. I'm not going to get into the specifics as we're focusing on Jimmy Page but basically these women were magickal conduits. For the Crowley followers out there, yes, I'm simplifying things as I don't want to stray too far off topic.

In relation to Jimmy Page, the opportunities to find his own Scarlet Women and experiment were copious given his status as a rock star. JP's view on women was seemingly influenced by Crowley as evidenced by this surprising quote.

> 'Crowley didn't have a very high opinion of women and I don't think he was wrong. Playing music is a very high sexual act. It's an emotional release and the sexual drive comes in along with all the other impulses.'

A very interesting comment and I suppose it could be interpreted in a number of ways. Curiously enough and it may just be a coincidence, but at the time of this writing, the old rock god is dating a girl 46 years (!) his junior who is named Scarlett. Does Jimmy Page seek out women named Scarlet or do women named Scarlet try to get his attention knowing that the name triggers his interest because of the Crowley connection? However, the current Scarlett isn't the only one. Scarlet Lilith Page was born on March 24th, 1971. Now there's no way it's a coincidence that JP named his daughter Scarlet Lilith given that these names are significant in relation to occultism and Aleister Crowley.

We know about Scarlet Women but what about the name Lilith? Lilith is a figure in Jewish mythology known as a dangerous demon of the night. She is sexually wanton and steals babies. In one of Crowley's technical books, De Arte Magica, Lilith appears as a succubus (female demon that has sex with sleeping men) and was also one of the middle names of Crowley's first child. What am I getting at with this?

It further demonstrates the influence Aleister Crowley had and likely still has on Jimmy Page. The fact that Jimmy Page gave his daughter these two very significant occultic names is indicative of how important the ritual aspect (not just the research) of magick was/is to him as well as its (likely) continued influence given the name of the woman he's currently dating. Yes, I'm aware that for some of you this will be a stretch but for others it will be quite an obvious connection.

There are all sorts of crazy JP groupie stories and most interesting among them is his penchant for whipping the girls. TV star John Stamos once played with JP at a charity concert event. During an interview with Howard Stern, Stamos stated that in JP's hotel room he saw whips and 'devil stuff' in the rock star's suitcase. Why would Jimmy Page be travelling with whips? The whole whips thing is mentioned rather consistently and has been referenced by JP's most prominent groupies during interviews or in their books.

Whipping is used during rituals for a variety of purposes but at the core this technique is used to focus consciousness as pinpoint focus is absolutely critical to bridge the gap between the physical and nonphysical worlds. Priests are often depicted whipping themselves 'for God' or because they feel guilt or not worthy, etc. but in reality it's all a prompting from the nonphysical (via demonic consciousness) to open a small portal, a fissure if you will, into the physical plane. So why was Jimmy Page whipping groupies in hotel rooms? He may have been performing specific rituals or he may have been getting off on the combination of pain and pleasure the girls were feeling which is a sign of demonic influence. Sure; he could have been just trying freaky stuff for fun but given his occult background this is highly unlikely.

Whenever someone likes inflicting pain upon another person trust me, there's a dark entity present. Once again, these sharp bursts of pain create a doorway into the physical world so that nonphysical beings can gain access to the energy fields of the living and experience all of the stuff (sex, food, etc.) they cannot from their frequency of existence. So my best guess is that Page had entities around him that impulsed the whipping in conjunction with other sexual activities which all opened a doorway for these spirits to enter his body. And what spirit doesn't want to inhabit the body of a rich, hedonistic rock star worshipped by millions? Yes, lot's of speculation there but I told you we'd be doing that. Now let's talk about curses…

5 The Curse- Statues of Gold

In the introduction we discussed the legend of the Led Zeppelin Curse potentially being the result of Jimmy Page's occult interest leading to the band's (alleged) pact with the Devil. We also referenced the curse put upon Page by experimental filmmaker Kenneth Anger. In the previous two chapters we went over the occult symbolism and (possible) rituals Page injected Led Zeppelin's recorded music and performances with. In this chapter we will discuss who Kenneth Anger is, how he met Jimmy Page and what led Anger to curse the rock star.

Kenneth Anger- the name says it all, doesn't it? Like Page, Anger is an occultist and devotee of Aleister Crowley. He is also an underground filmmaker and author. I'll give you a sense of this guy's vibe. He's got a large tattoo across his chest that reads 'Lucifer'. Look him up online; he's a scary looking dude and I know Anger would just love hearing that description of him. But to be fair, Lucifer means different things to different people. Anger began making short films at ten years old and has produced almost forty since 1937 with the predominant themes being homoeroticism and the occult. His imagery is surreal and Anger himself has called his films invocations and rituals.

He was born Kenneth Wilbur Anglemyer in California in 1927. Curiously enough, the words angel and angle are connected. The word Angle of the Anglo-Saxons means divine messenger and Anger was born with the name Anglemyer and then his life became defined by the original angel, Lucifer. This is a neat synchronicity and synchronistic events play a big part in all things magick.

Anger claimed to have been a child actor notably appearing in the film A Midsummer Night's Dream and would later write the gossip book Hollywood Babylon which contained many juicy stories of scandal among old school film stars. He would later be described as one of America's first openly gay filmmakers whose work unflinchingly addressed homosexuality and gay culture. Being an adherent of Thelema, the religion that Aleister Crowley founded, his films focus on occult themes with notable titles such as Invocation of My Demon Brother and Lucifer Rising; the latter being pivotal in this story.

During his life Anger mixed with the rich and famous; among them counterculture figures, writers and rock stars such as Tennessee Williams, Mick Jagger, Keith Richards, Marianne Faithfull and Anton Lavey (no surprise there). He also struck up a friendship with pioneering (and some would say notorious) 'sexologist' Alfred Kinsey who was one of the fist people to buy a copy of Anger's film, Fireworks. This movie was a shocker for its time and would get Anger arrested on obscenity charges. Fireworks explored themes such as homosexuality and sadomasochism and had some pretty bizarre and violent imagery.

In 1955 Anger and sexologist Kinsey travelled to the derelict Abbey of Thelema in Sicily which, as discussed earlier, was used as a commune of debauchery by Aleister Crowley in the 1920's. They made the trip to film a documentary titled Thelema Abbey for the British television series Omnibus. While there,

Anger restored many of the villa's sexually themed wall paintings and also performed Crowleyan rituals. And of course years later Jimmy Page would visit the Abbey so it seems this creepy place, along with Boleskine House, has a strange pull for those who follow Crowley.

Anger met Jimmy Page in 1971 at a Sotheby's auction of Aleister Crowley artifacts and they struck up a friendship based on their mutual interests. Around 1973 Page would invite Anger to Boleskine House to perform an exorcism as he was experiencing some ghostly disturbances. Curiously enough, Anger had rented Boleskine House for a brief period in 1969 before JP had purchased it in 1970.

Understanding the significance of Boleskine House and the occult rituals performed there by Aleister Crowley, it's almost certain that Kenneth Anger conducted rituals of his own which would anchor his energy to the property and give him remote access via the astral plane long after he left the haunted manor. Trust me; this is definitely something an occultist like Anger would do as it would amplify his magickal power and allow him to affect the place itself and those in it from a distance. I'm not saying that Anger marked his territory specifically because he knew Page was going to buy the house but it all worked out rather conveniently as so often happens with magick.

In any event, Anger and Page then agreed to collaborate on Anger's film Lucifer Rising. Page was to compose the soundtrack and come up with some unique music to go along with Anger's surreal imagery. Page worked on the soundtrack intermittently while touring the world with Led Zeppelin. In 1976 JP allowed Anger to edit his raw footage in the basement of the musician's London home which was originally fitted out to edit the concert film The Song Remains the Same. Page gave Anger free reign to use his subterranean film laboratory to trim the initial seventeen hours of raw footage down to roughly one and a half hours.

The first reports were that JP's live-in girlfriend Charlotte had discovered Anger giving unauthorized tours of their home and demanded that he leave. The filmmaker supposedly returned the next morning to collect his belongings and found the door bolted. The movie footage as well as his prized 'Crown of Lucifer', which was supposedly made with rhinestones from a dress once worn by Mae West, were all still inside. Anger then informed the folks at Zeppelin's record label Swansong that the collaboration was off and Page was officially fired from the project. He was eventually able to collect his things (including the movie footage) over the next couple of days. JP claimed that a housekeeper, not Charlotte, had asked Anger to leave.

Anger later stated that he'd been unable to reach Page for months and that the rock star's dedication to the project had obviously waned. Additional griping from the filmmaker included that JP was behaving contradictory to the teachings of their mutual hero Aleister Crowley and that his demeanor was akin to a 'lunar landscape'. He said that communicating with Page was like trying to speak through thick plate glass. Anger went on to say that JP was dried up as a musician and didn't have anything left creatively, etc. You know; the usual stuff you say to someone when you're pissed at them. He also alluded to Page's heroin addiction by referencing his *affair with the white lady* and saying his behavior was very Jekyll and Hyde.

Either way, Page had the upper hand as he didn't need this pet project with a tempestuous character like Anger. It is important to note that Page did indeed produce over twenty minutes of music for the soundtrack but Anger said it wasn't enough and that what was presented was unusable. The filmmaker was so upset that he threw a curse and let everyone know about it. Curiously enough, this is when the majority (but not all) of Led Zeppelin's bad luck started.

In my opinion, curses are not very effective unless propelled by an appropriate level of toxic, malevolent emotion. Of course the technical aspect, the ceremony, has to be there but without vicious yet focused rage the results will be lackluster. There are many cultural systems that have their own specific approach to harming a person or group of people. There are certain ritualistic steps one must take which equate to a formula or recipe. But just as a successful chef injects love or positive energy into their meals (however immeasurable some might think this is) a Black Magician must inject hate into their curses for them to be truly effective. After their fallout, when asked if he felt vindictive towards Jimmy Page, Anger responded *'you bet I do; I'm not a Christian turn the other cheek kind.'* He also reportedly said with a smile, *'In fact, I'm all ready to throw a Kenneth Anger curse.'*

That quote says a lot about Anger; no pun intended. This guy is full of ego and vitriol. He had also been described as an impulsive nut job that could fly off the handle in the blink of an eye. This is all indicative of a person with demonic attachment; someone who has practiced dark rituals and has all sorts of creepy stuff in their energy field. However, I'm not judging Kenneth Anger as I've got firsthand experience with this and know the signs all too well. He's obviously a talented artist but messing with the occult usually gets the better of everyone.

Anger bitterly recalled that *'he and Charlotte (JP's girlfriend) had so many servants yet they would never offer me a cup of tea or a sandwich which is such a mistake on their part because I put the Curse of King Midas on them. If you're greedy and just amass gold you'll get an illness so I turned her and Jimmy Page into statues of gold.'* Anger obviously took the lack of offering tea and sandwiches as inhospitable but we really don't know the specific circumstances. The fact that he cites this as an example of behavior warranting a curse is another indication of spirit attachment. People that react disproportionately to being slighted are under the influence, so to speak. I know because it's a weakness of mine as well which is connected to messing with demons.

In response to Anger's comments on this incident Page described it all as pathetic and said he considered returning Anger's possessions in a hearse but thought it might be too dramatic. JP also said that the curse 'just' consisted of silly letters that Anger was writing and sending to everyone that Anger thought Page knew so they would bring it up in conversation. However, silly or not, JP didn't realize the power of getting other minds to vibrate in that direction (by reading the letters and commenting on them). Anger knew what he was doing. Also; fame and its ability to amplify things surely played a part.

Furthermore; Page dismissively said that the only damage Anger could do is with his tongue. Ah; but the tongue is all-powerful when it comes to magick. Another of JP's comments on the matter was that Lucifer Rising was going to be a masterpiece but Anger didn't pull it off. So we had a little tit for tat going on between these two which is standard for magickal collisions. There's always drama following conflict and even more so when the occult is involved.

In regards to the Curse of King Midas, Anger is referring to the ancient story about the tragedy of greed which illustrates what happens when true happiness is not recognized or appreciated. There are several versions of this Greek myth but the gist of it is that Midas was rewarded by the God Dionysus for treating his satyr (part man, part goat) with kindness and offered to grant the king a wish for his good deed. Midas requested that everything he touched be turned to gold. Dionysus asked if the king was absolutely sure that he wanted this. Midas didn't hesitate in confirming that was indeed what he wanted.

Of course this was a handy ability; at least initially. After turning a few otherwise useful things such as fruit and a chariot into gold he excitedly reached for his daughter's hand to show her what he could do and then realized that his child was now a life-sized golden statue. Fortunately, Dionysus was kind enough to reverse this magic touch as Midas painfully realized it was more of a curse than a blessing.

So what was the goal of Anger's hex on Jimmy Page? From an occult perspective, the Curse of King Midas is a metaphor for sickness or impotence despite enormous fame and wealth. Anger cleverly reinforced his intentions with the curse by commenting that Page was dried up as a musician and that his creativity was tapped. Well sure enough, from that point forward (and even to this day) Jimmy Page has been in a creative coma. He's got all the money in the world but hasn't successfully moved on from Zeppelin as the two remaining members of the band have done. Of course this is all subjective and one could argue that JP has done other significant musical work but the consensus is that he, as such a talented artist, could be doing so much more. We'll discuss this creative slump in detail shortly.

So in the end, Anger did complete Lucifer Rising but it left a messy wake of death and tragedy ultimately connecting to the Manson murders and the Rolling Stones' Altamont free concert disaster which we'll elaborate on later. However, the venture did result in a uniquely creepy piece of music by Jimmy Page which has since become quite a hot item. It is rumored that the beginning of the Zeppelin song In the Evening is taken from the soundtrack that Page came up with for Lucifer Rising; the piece of music which Anger ultimately rejected. I absolutely love it! Have a listen…

6 The Zeppelin Plummets

So what effect (if any) did all of Jimmy Page's occult dabbling and Kenneth Anger's cursing (he likely did more than one) have on Led Zeppelin? After all; that's why we're here, right? Your answer, my answer, everyone's answer is irrelevant because there is no way to prove such a thing. However, let's examine the unfortunate series of events and then decide whether or not there was a supernatural culprit.

Although whispers started behind the scenes in the mid 70's, the curse talk really picked up steam when rock journalists fed the flames tying three significant occurrences together. Robert Plant's 1975 car crash, his son's tragic and mysterious death in 1977 and then John Bonham's death in 1980 were the key events that gave birth to the Led Zeppelin Curse.

Sure; previous to this, unfortunate things happened to Zeppelin from time-to-time that could easily be chalked up to everyday life. However, from 1975 forward, bad luck enveloped the band on a regular basis. An ominous black cloud followed them everywhere they went. Let's have a look.

In March of 1975, during their North American tour, a woman from Charles Manson's family confronted an executive of Zeppelin's record company urgently demanding to speak with Jimmy Page. VP Danny Goldberg, sensing it was best to placate this seeming nutter, asked her to write down a message for JP and then said he'd get it to him the following night. Lynne 'Squeaky' Fromme wrote a long note but said the next night would probably be too late as she needed to warn Jimmy Page of the 'bad energy' which put him in imminent danger. She claimed to be able to see the future and that the last time this happened she saw someone killed before her very eyes. Squeaky finally went away and the note was allegedly burned; never to be read.

An important detail is that in September of the same year, just six months after requesting an audience with Jimmy Page, Squeaky Fromme was arrested for attempting to assassinate then-president Gerald Ford. She pointed a gun at him, dressed in a red robe no less! She was obviously a crazy person but this illustrates the type of energy that had Jimmy Page on its radar. Unstable people like our girl Squeaky are used as vessels by demonic energies as their mental imbalances allow for easy infiltration.

A harbinger of Fromme's spooky visit came in January, just before the band's departure to the US. Jimmy Page broke his left ring finger in a train door. It could have been any type of injury but it was his finger; a guitarist's most vital asset. Jimmy was forced to take pain killers (I'm sure he had no issue with that) and developed a three-finger playing technique during the tour to compensate for the injury.

As the tour kicked off, Robert Plant got a bad flu which plagued him over many performances and contributed to some notably bad reviews. Then of course we had Squeaky Fromme's timely, stalkerish appearance which triggered the bad luck dam to crack as then John Bonham became ill with a stomach disorder and repeatedly lost his drum sticks.

There was also a frightening incident where a heavy amplifier mysteriously fell, almost causing serious injury. These relatively small occurrences alone can easily be written off as a rough patch for Zeppelin and everybody has those. After all, the boogeyman can't be blamed for everything. However, with Squeaky Fromme's ominous visit sandwiched in there you can almost feel the cold creep in; as if there's something even bigger around the corner.

The second leg of Zeppelin's 75' US tour ended a short time after the Manson girl's warning. Then the band took a scheduled break following a series of shows in London. There were more concerts planned but they were all cancelled. On Monday August 4th, 1975 Plant and his family were on holiday in Rhodes, Greece when they were in a terrible car accident. The lead singer and his wife were seriously injured and had to be airlifted back to London for treatment. Plant suffered multiple fractures of the ankle, foot and elbow. Plant's then-wife, Maureen, had concussions, several breaks in her leg, four fractures of the pelvis and bad facial lacerations. Their four year old son suffered a fractured leg as well as cuts and bruises. Their daughter had a broken wrist, cuts and bruises. As you can see, this was a serious accident and could have easily gotten everyone in that car killed.

Jimmy Page and his family were also on this trip with the Plants but on August 3rd Jimmy left to check on some real estate in Sicily. Page's partner was in a different vehicle but his daughter, Scarlet, was in the car with the Plants. Miraculously, Scarlet was unharmed. Can you believe it? Five people in that car and four out of the five suffered some pretty serious injuries; all except for Scarlet Page. In no way shape or form am I suggesting that Jimmy Page's occult dabbling was responsible for this accident.

However, JP's professed use of Talismanic magick may have spared his daughter injury as her genetics and energy field are connected to his and the protection / magick may have shielded her. Hey, it can't be proven but it also can't be disproven. Think about it; statistically speaking, she should have been hurt.

So JP broke away just a day before this major accident to check out some real estate in Sicily. Did he receive some sort of subconscious premonition or warning which prompted this timely side-trip? Also; where did he go again? What's in Sicily? Do you remember Aleister Crowley's Abbey of Thelema from chapter two? JP allegedly traveled there with Benji Lefevre who was a vocal technician, audio engineer and producer. Lefevre's main focus while with the band was as Robert Plant's vocal assistant.

Jimmy Page was considering the acquisition of Crowley's temple of debauchery but for some reason it never happened. However, he was there and I suspect that this energy is somehow connected to and maybe worked in conjunction with JP's own magick to help him avoid the accident and also help Scarlet emerge uninjured. But then again; with the occult you never really know what you're dealing with and it usually requires something in return or ricochets. Regarding the Plants' misfortune, it's quite possible (and I emphasize possible) that the negative energy which was following the band around and couldn't get through Jimmy Page's defenses had a residual effect on those he was most recently with. There are innumerable possibilities when the invisible world is summoned to pierce the veil and affect / assist the physical.

Now some of you may have picked up on the fact that Kenneth Anger cursed Page (and by association Led Zeppelin) in 1976 yet the car accident occurred in 1975. During my research I found several articles dating the car crash to 1976 to conveniently fit in with the curse theory. However, just because the one public curse happened a year later doesn't necessarily mean that Kenneth Anger wasn't involved.

As discussed earlier, magick does not always work in a linear fashion and is not bound by the time constraints of the physical world. The key is that Anger was already in Zeppelin's orbit by the time of the Greece accident. I'll elaborate on this in my conclusions chapter but suffice to say that I'm aware of this seeming inconsistency.

Plant's recovery was slow and painful. He spent a great deal of time in a wheelchair and of course was unable to tour. The accident also delayed work on their next LP, titled Presence. Plant ultimately recorded the album from his wheelchair and it was released in March 1976.

While the singer was convalescing, the first in a string of Zeppelin-related 1970's deaths occurred. Best known for being the lead vocalist of the Yardbirds, Keith Relf died on May 14th, 1976. Jimmy Page was with the Yardbirds before forming Led Zeppelin. Relf electrocuted himself in his basement while playing an improperly earthed (electrically grounded) guitar. Accident? Maybe.

I'm going to keep everything in sequence so you can see the progression of events beginning with the 1975 tour which we've already covered. I'll continue with occurrences directly related to the band as well as tragedy peripherally connected to Zeppelin so that everything lines up chronologically.

Next is the October 1976 Page and Anger brouhaha which we discussed in a previous chapter. The temperamental filmmaker was ejected from Page's London home resulting in the 'big' public curse which was by no means (in my opinion) the only source of negative occultic energy which affected the band.

When they finally got back on the road the bad luck continued. Led Zeppelin's 1977 North American tour was their eleventh and final tour on that side of the pond. Performances were scheduled to commence on 27 February in Texas but Plant contracted laryngitis and the tour was delayed for a month. It ultimately kicked off on April 1st which is not exactly a lucky date.

Because of the initial delay, all of the band's equipment had already been shipped to America which left them unable to rehearse and they were understandably rusty. Jimmy Page hadn't played his guitar for over a month and said he was terrified to go out onstage. As an aside; JP wore his custom-made white silk dragon suit on this tour. The famous outfit was also known as the 'Poppy White Dragon Suit' likely coined due to Page's raging heroin addiction which we'll discuss in a few moments.

However, despite the first couple of setbacks this turned out to be one of Zeppelin's most successful tours ever as they broke both financial and attendance records on April 30th in Detroit, Michigan. I can see King Midas in the background; arms folded and shaking his head. Yes, there was plenty of gold for one of the greatest rock bands ever but there was also blood; lots of it.

Ticketless fans at a sold out Cincinnati show went crazy and started a riot which resulted in many injuries and over seventy arrests. This particular location was also the same place where eleven fans were trampled to death at a Who performance just two years later. It sounds to me like the chaos energy from the Zeppelin show lingered and was reactivated as time and vibration do not operate on the same frequency. In Tampa Florida an open-air concert had to be cut short due to a massive thunderstorm. A riot broke out at that one too resulting in fifty injuries and nineteen arrests. It was so bad that tear gas had to be used to break up the melee.

At a Chicago concert Page was so sick that he had to play one song from a chair and then the show was prematurely ended due to this illness. The official word was food poisoning. It seems that a great deal of jagged energy was swirling around the band, following them from show to show and slowly closing in.

Then one of the most infamous and savage incidents in Zeppelin's history occurred on July 23rd in Oakland, California. The band's manager Peter Grant, drummer John Bonham and their hired muscle, London gangster John Bindon assaulted one of the promoter's backstage staff. It seems that Grant's eleven year old son, Warren, attempted to remove a sign that was needed for the following night's performance and was told no by the staff member. This allegedly got back to Grant in a slightly different manner via a trouble-stirring Bonham. Grant thought his son was treated more harshly than he actually was and went berserk.

At this point Grant was deeply into cocaine which amplified his notorious hair-trigger temper. As a result, the promoter's employee was beaten so badly that he had to be hospitalized. The next day a SWAT team surrounded their hotel and arrested Grant, Bindon and Bonham. Also arrested was Zeppelin tour manager Richard Cole as he was standing guard during the beating. All four narrowly escaped serious charges and jail time, ultimately receiving suspended sentences and fines. As you can see, things were getting progressively messier for the world's greatest rock band.

After the beating incident and considerable drama Zeppelin played a second Oakland concert which would end up being their final live appearance in the United States. On July 26th just after arriving in New Orleans, Plant received the news that his son had fallen ill with a mystery virus. He then received another call with the devastating news that his son had passed away. The tour was immediately cancelled and Plant went into seclusion to heal. Led Zeppelin's future was again up in the air.

Years later Plant described the chaos they dealt with on that 1977 tour. He said that it was 'insane' and there was 'no way of containing the energy in those buildings'. Jack Calmes (interesting name, given what he's addressing) was the head of the company that provided the sound, lights and staging for Zeppelin's American tours in the mid seventies. He described the incredible amount of tension on that tour and said that it was the darkest, most negative Zeppelin tour ever. He thought the drugs and thugs were a factor as hard core gangsters like the aforementioned John Bindon were brought in by manager Peter Grant to act as security guards. Of course violence and drugs magnetize dark entities and we'll discuss that shortly.

Ok; so you may be thinking that although tragic, these events cannot be definitively attributed to a curse. Fair enough; I totally agree with you. However, there's even more. Earlier we discussed how notorious occultist Aleister Crowley found his way onto the Beatles' Sgt. Pepper album. Crowley also popped up in connection with another, less-known band. English group Eddie and the Hot Rod wrote a tune that was inspired by Crowley's dictum 'Do What Thou Wilt Shall be the Whole of the Law'.

If you recall from an earlier chapter, Do What Thou Wilt was pressed into the outtro groove of Led Zeppelin III under JP's direction. This phrase was obviously very important to JP and he took the meaning of it quite seriously. The title of the song by Eddie and the Hot Rod was Do Anything You Wanna Do which is exactly how this Crowley phrase is most often misinterpreted.

The song was released on July 29th, 1977 just days after Robert Plant's son died. Can you imagine how pissed off Jimmy Page must have been? Look at the timing. Led Zeppelin had just come off a rough, tragedy-laden tour and the band's future was up in the air. Then this flippant song is released rubbing salt into JP's wounds. Do What Thou Wilt basically means find your true purpose and put all of your energy into it versus wasting your life on the goals and desires society imposes on you which just creates misery. It doesn't mean do anything you want regardless of the consequences or who you might hurt in the process.

Do Anything You Wanna Do reached the Top Ten. The band put Crowley on the cover of the single but wanted to lighten things up (Crowley's photos are pretty intense after all) by putting a pair of Mickey Mouse ears on the old occultist's head. Apparently Jimmy Page found out and allegedly placed a curse of his own on Eddie and the Hot Rods for insulting Crowley. As previously discussed, curses don't necessarily work in a dramatic death and explosion-laced way. Curses sometimes perpetuate themselves as well. Quite often the cursed are prone to cursing others.

So what happened to Eddie and the Hot Rod? The band was soon dropped from their label, their manager became hooked on heroin (addiction is synonymous with demonic attachment) and they pretty much sputtered out. The band's base player even said that weird stuff happened and the general consensus was that they shouldn't have messed with Aleister Crowley. You'll notice that his comment about 'weird stuff' indicates that there was more than the record label drop and heroin addiction. There is always more when it comes to the misuse of spiritual energy; not just the overt things that may or may not make the news, etc.

If JP did indeed curse Eddie and the Hot Rod it wouldn't be surprising. Even if he never practiced any so-called black magick previously, it's all too easy to become impulsive and vindictive when you're swimming in those waters. I think the key here is the timing as JP must have been in a foul mood following the 77' tour.

Let's say that Jimmy Page summoned demons from the Goetia spell book/grimoire (the one he had specially reprinted through his occult bookstore) just to see if they were real, just out of curiosity. If this is true then the demons would have easily gotten their hooks into him. Once again, how can you spend the effort and money to reprint a particular book with such care and attention to detail and not test it? It's like reproducing an ancient cookbook and not trying out one of the recipes. Remember, JP only reprinted two books through his shop; Goetia and a book on astrology.

When the occult bug bit me I was so excited to summon a demon and communicate with it. I had no intention of casting a spell or employing one of the spirits to hurt people. I just wanted to be in the presence of something dangerous and ominous; very much like the desire to do a cage dive with a White Shark. Trust me; nobody just 'researches' magick. If by some small chance Jimmy Page never practiced Goetia rituals; just that kind of a connection with the book, reprinting it, would put him on their radar. Furthermore; Kenneth Anger's curse would have put him at an even higher risk of demonic attachment and maybe possession.

This type of energy can create impulsive, rage-filled thoughts and reactions from the slightest agitation. Kenneth Anger himself is a great example. He is well known for a hair-trigger temper and vengeful behavior. Now add the copious drugs and alcohol Jimmy Page was consuming and you've got the perfect setting for being 'nudged' by spirits. It's a slippery slope and even the most experienced occultists are very vulnerable to spirit attachment and possession.

However, we have to balance the speculation, the things we cannot prove, along with the more overt stuff like untimely deaths. That being said; I do agree that if you look at just about any person's history you could find evidence of a curse if you really wanted to. You could point at so-and-so's car crash or a string of accidents and suicides, etc. as 'strange' and possibly indicative of something unnatural. Then connect their great auntie's penchant for reading palms or tea leaves and bang, you've got a curse. This is what the more scientific, statistically oriented folk would say in regards to curses in general and certainly the Led Zeppelin Curse. Fair enough; that could very well be the case but let's have a look at some more of the untimely deaths connected to the band.

Keith Harwood died on September 3rd, 1977. He was a recording engineer that worked on a number of Zeppelin albums including Houses of the Holy, Physical Graffiti and Presence. Keith fell asleep at the wheel and hit a tree on his way home from mixing sessions. He was allegedly on heroin at the time of the accident. Keith had also worked with the Rolling Stones who were connected to Kenneth Anger as well and we'll explore that particular connection later. Coincidence? Just an accident? Sure; possibly.

Folk singer Sandy Denny (who accompanied Robert Plant on the Zeppelin song Battle of Evermore) died on 21 April, 1978 after head injuries sustained from a tumble down her parents' stairs. Another random occurrence? Maybe. By the way; Sandy also had her own symbol/sigil on Led Zeppelin IV. Check it out.

Photographer Phillip Hale died in October of 1979. Hale was partying with Jimmy Page at his Plumpton, England mansion and overdosed on heroin. Deaths and accidents happen in life but when they pile up like this you have to wonder.

Magick is notorious for completely backfiring, working in a time-lapse fashion or basically manifesting in a way not intended by the magician. I'll give you a brief example. The great electrical scientist Nikola Tesla was depicted in the 2006 film The Prestige. Hugh Jackman's character, a stage magician, commissioned Tesla to build a magic box/trick for him. The box was supposed to teleport the magician but it worked in a way that Tesla (also historically known as The Wizard of the West) did not intend. Instead of teleporting the magic box's occupant it duplicated/cloned them!

Tesla saw this as a dangerous failure and recommended that Jackman's character drop it to the bottom of the ocean. Do you think this advice was followed? I shared this film analogy to demonstrate an example of what happens far too often in the occult world. If you haven't seen The Prestige I highly recommend it!

Sure, there are deaths aplenty connected to the Zeppelin Curse but the main target / focal point seems to have gotten off scott-free. Well, not exactly. The results of a curse can be a slow burn as well. Jimmy Page's heroin addiction is a smoking gun. The majority consensus was that JP's playing ability suffered significantly from his heavy smack use starting around 1975. I suspect that some sort of magickal working occurred at or around this time. Whether it was by Page, Kenneth Anger or the both of them doing spells separately is anyone's guess. Remember that Robert Plant's car accident in Greece occurred in 75' too.

With heroin you go into such a deep, dreamlike state that you can be 'worked on' more effectively by spiritual tapeworms or soul infections. During JP's long-term heroin stupor I'm sure that many astral beings permanently grafted themselves onto his energy field. The addiction certainly stifled his creativity which we'll discuss shortly. Also; this sort of vampiric slow-drain is covert and actually more beneficial to the demon / malevolent spirit in the long run as it ensures a consistent stream of food (life force) and access to physical pleasures (via subtle possession) than a one-off car accident or impulsed suicide, etc.

It really depends on the type of entity involved and how they access the target which is often determined by that individual's weaknesses. Openings in the energy field which spirits can see via their perspective from the astral plane often correlate with physical and/or neurochemical deficiencies as they are interconnected.

What was around Page (and is likely still there) never really goes away. Sure, he's off the drugs now but it's too late as the spirits have burrowed their way into his energy field. This is not the Hollywood, head-spinning, pea soup type of possession. It's the permanent type that is very subtle and only might (just might) be apparent to those very close to the target.

When it comes to spirit infiltration, the real deal is all around us and happens a lot more than you'd think. This is creepy stuff and the machinations of nonphysical beings aren't very often exposed because people are too distracted and don't want to see what's right in front of and inside them.

What! Who am I to suggest that Jimmy Page is possessed? As I've said from the beginning, I'm only speculating based on the information that I have and knowing what he's exposed himself to. Owning Aleister Crowley's former home (regardless of how little time he allegedly spent there) and reprinting the Goetia certainly qualify him for possession. The overt behavior like having to finish a song on a stool or mumbling incoherently through an interview is indicative of a struggle.

Once the entity wins and becomes entrenched the target goes back to normal and carries on with their life; albeit with a permanent resident. Some struggle longer than others and some do shake that monkey off their backs but I think JP still has his and I'm sure many would (silently) agree with me. I can hear some of you now- *it's ridiculous to suggest such a thing!* Maybe initially but why is it such a stretch given what he's been into? Also remember that real possession is only very, very rarely spinning heads and pea soup. Either way it's something to consider.

Some of you might be wondering why Jimmy Page didn't act like John Bonham? Why wasn't he tearing apart hotel rooms and beating people bloody? Two reasons- everyone responds differently (based on their own personal genetic makeup) to their energy field being opened up by mind altering substances and the type of substance will also be a factor.

Despite being a depressant alcohol tends to trigger aggression whereas opiates like heroin draw one further inward. Possession can take place in both scenarios but the type of entity (or entities) that grafts onto a host can vary. Yes; Page and Bonham both consumed alcohol, heroin and likely a plethora of other substances but each had their preferred drugs and were thus invaded by the astral based on the main effects of each.

John Bonham's alcoholism and erratic behavior were highly indicative of malevolent occult energy swirling about the band which could have been the result of a curse. Out of all the band members, John Bonham seemed to be the most easily manipulated by the demons circling the group. Yes; alcoholism has been around forever and yes, spirit attachment has always been connected to this addiction but given the fact that Zeppelin has been in the public eye and their exploits documented so thoroughly we can examine the clues in detail. Regarding the alcohol / spirit connection; why do you think hard alcohol like whiskey is called a spirit?

Of course Bonham was a drinker before he met Jimmy Page but his already simmering alcoholism was seized upon by the entities that flocked to the band due to JP's occult practice and/or Kenneth Anger's involvement. What exacerbated things was the fact that the public knew JP was into the occult (post Zeppelin 3) and just the thought of it, by thousands of fans, would pull in additional entities and create more potent reverberations. Collective mind power cannot be underestimated. Part of the reason we see such bizarre and erratic behavior from celebrities is due to the sheer number of people focusing on them. By the way, it doesn't matter whether or not you consistently practice magick or just 'research' it; the entities come to you regardless.

Bonham was notorious for staying up all night and destroying hotel rooms, causing fights and all sorts of other aggressive behavior. He's pulled guns on people and even once punched the lights out of a female journalist for just looking at him and smiling. He's torn apart backstage catering setups, punched holes in walls and even ripped a car to pieces with his bare hands.

Eventually, the rest of the band steered clear of him when not onstage. They stayed on different floors of the hotel to keep away from Bonham's nightly tsunami of destruction. Sure, a degree of this is all good fun and generally typical rock star behavior but given the level of severity and in the context of nearby occult practice and a potential curse it's definitely not.

The stock standard responses to Bonzo's behavior were that he was homesick, had stage fright, didn't like flying, etc. His antics were downplayed by everyone, especially Jimmy Page, and for good reason. Nobody wants to tarnish the legacy of Zeppelin. As for JP, the band was and still is his baby. He can't wait to get out there and tour again but Plant is being a rock-block...more on that later. Bonham was by all accounts a kind, generous person when he wasn't boozing. However, his personality shifted majorly when on the piss and that's what I'm getting at.

His predisposition for being an extra-open vessel when altered really illuminated just how infested with entities Zeppelin was. Lots of rock bands are; it comes with the territory. Fame (and the amplifying collective mental focus it brings) substance abuse and definitely all of the sexual energy circulating from groupies makes this possible. However, the effect was on a whole different level when it came to Led Zeppelin.

With Bonham it was more like lower level astral garbage (thought forms and volatile parasitic spirits) did the old hit and run thing when he was plastered. He'd be really drunk and then get infested and impulsed to act out and then be fine in the morning only to repeat the cycle after the next performance.

With Jimmy Page, due to his main drug being heroin, I think that more intelligent and truly dark beings were anchored to him. By this I mean demonic forces that are more whole and able to think and ultimately make a plan for long term possession versus the turbulent and less coherent stuff that plagued Bonham. Another factor was of course that JP was actually practicing magick whereas Bonham was not.

Some of you might be wondering how bassist John Paul Jones escaped the black cloud of the Led Zeppelin Curse. The myth tells us that the more pragmatic 'Jonsey' didn't partake in the deal with the Devil ritual that the other three allegedly engaged in. However, I think the answer is more complex (and yet paradoxically simple) than that. Some people are invisible and/or inaccessible to the astral realm. Their agenda for a particular lifetime might not involve interfacing (whether consciously or unconsciously) with the nonphysical. I'm sure, given that Jones seems to be a quiet and contemplative type that he has detailed theories on the Led Zeppelin Curse but wisely keeps them to himself.

The event that crystallized the Led Zeppelin Curse took place on September 25th, 1980. While rehearsals were underway for a comeback North American tour, John Bonham died in his sleep. He choked on his own vomit after a day-long drinking binge. Like photographer Philip Hale, Bonham died in one of Page's homes. This time it was the Old Mill House in Clewer, Windsor. Could these be sacrifices claimed by the demons? Was the occultic energy possibly seeking payment for JP's protection or was it Kenneth Anger's curse? Another curious synchronicity was that Benji Lefevre, the Zeppelin assistant and sound technician, was the one who found Bonham dead. If you recall, Lefevre accompanied Jimmy Page to the Abbey of Thelema in Sicily back in 1975. I'm not suggesting anything except that magick and synchronicity go hand-in-hand. I'll let you draw your own conclusions there.

The media seized upon Page's occult connections and of course, as they always do, twisted the truth to sensationalize things. They spoke of Jimmy Page's interest in the dark side of the supernatural; particularly séances, practicing black magic and satanic rituals. This all became part of the mystical rumors that swirled around Led Zeppelin. Coincidentally (or not); Manson girl Lynette 'Squeaky' Fromme foresaw the bad energy headed Zeppelin's way and tried to warn them all. Like it or not, the media never forgets.

Ultimately, regardless of whether or not one believes that Anger's curse or Jimmy Page's occult dabbling had some effect on the band, their fortunes certainly hit a plateau and then began a slow plummet in 1975. Some of the more obvious things like Bonham's death, JP's heroin addiction or Plant's crash in Rhodes and his personal tragedy might point towards a curse's effectiveness. However, think about the more subtle things, the occurrences that were written or talked about publicly but not really connected by journalists looking to sensationalize the band's misfortune. These are the less dramatic events that might have been hidden in plain view.

Finally we have the day-to-day things that would never be heard about in the media which might cumulatively lend to the effectiveness of a curse. What am I talking about? What small, daily effects could a curse have? Things like minor injuries; say to one of Page's fingers (which really happened) or perhaps a fall or maybe a fight with a band mate or groupie. Maybe he has a really bad nightmare (which is often indicative of entity presence) or is in just a horrid, depressed mood, etc. These and similar symptoms can be the residual effects of a curse. What most folks don't realize is that just because a curse doesn't result in an immediate fiery car crash, loss of limb in a piece of machinery or death from a mystery virus doesn't mean that the curse didn't work. Because magickal operations (positive or negative) don't necessarily adhere to linear time or follow straight paths they are hard to track/confirm.

Kenneth Anger said he put the Curse of King Midas on Jimmy Page; the effects of which can be interpreted as disease or impotence. What happened to Page's music career after John Bonham died and the band broke up? We've discussed the accidents and deaths but the slow creep of creative impotence, despite continued wealth and fame, may very well indicate that Anger was successful. We'll get into that as well as Zeppelin's many reunion attempts in the next chapter.

7 The Reunion That Wasn't

On September 25th, 1980 the original Led Zeppelin was no more. John Bonham had died and the remaining band members said they could not carry on as they were. Since then Robert Plant has gone on to release five original albums and has toured a great deal. John Paul Jones has also had a busy post-Zeppelin life both performing and working in the studio with other bands. They have moved on which is the ideal scenario after a significant loss. Of course there will be a mourning period following a tragedy like Bonham's passing but the healthy, natural thing to do is continue living. Some take longer than others and occasionally there are those that just stop.

They say that an artist's lifeblood is their creativity and seeing the manifestation of those creative endeavors. Robert Plant and John Paul Jones continued on but did Jimmy Page? No, not really. Of course some people can't easily adjust after a sudden void is created in their lives and it's certainly understandable but was Jimmy Page's inertia natural?

'I've done far worse than kill you. I've hurt you. And I wish to go on hurting you. I shall leave you as you left me, marooned for all eternity!'

Where did that come from? It's an adapted quote from Star Trek 2, The Wrath of Khan. I've included this because it sounds like something Kenneth Anger might have wanted to say to Jimmy Page over the years as he's tried to get back on track creatively and also reform Led Zeppelin. Jimmy Page is Captain Kirk and Kenneth Anger is Khan, the marooned bad boy. As we discussed earlier there are differing opinions regarding what happened with JP's effort on the Lucifer Rising soundtrack.

Although Anger fired Page I'm sure he felt marooned by JP's waning interest in a project that was extremely important to him. Some say that a tortured life is far, far worse

The Reunion That Wasn't

than the prospect of death. Maybe that was Anger's plan for Jimmy Page all along; to go on hurting him...a statue of gold, remember?

The purpose of this chapter is to demonstrate that the Led Zeppelin Curse, whatever its origin may be, didn't complete its objective on September 25th, 1980 but lives on to torment Jimmy Page. He may be incredibly wealthy and famous but JP has been in purgatory since Zeppelin crashed. He's been unable to move forward (to any significant degree) creatively and all of his attempts to bring the remaining members of the group back together have sputtered and failed.

Following John Bonham's death Page went into seclusion, continued his heroin habit and then putted about for years, getting involved in small projects here and there. For someone like Jimmy Page, a music industry veteran, this is decidedly unusual. Yes he eventually worked on the soundtrack to the movie Death Wish 2 and then there was the modestly successful group The Firm but something's not right there. Once again, a curse does not necessarily have to result in overtly destructive and dramatic events. There can be moderate effects that pick away at a target over time.

Another factor is that curses, or any focused release of energy for that matter, do not necessarily follow a linear, time-constrained path. Once a curse is projected out into the universe it will try to manifest in the physical world regardless of time. For example, a centuries-old hex could circle the target seeking an opening forever; hunting that soul through innumerable life streams. Of course the malevolent energy will lose momentum if not regularly fortified by its creator or some sort of proxy like books or the media. Old curses that are regularly discussed, studied, read about, etc. carry on through the attention / mental focus they are given. The internet chatter about Jimmy Page and the Zeppelin Curse is very much akin to an archaeologist repeatedly entering the mummy's tomb and releasing the noxious mist. Ok; I'm guilty of that too…

Kenneth Anger, for lack of a better word, is an angry person and not one to forget a slight. Many years after the 1976 curse he had gone on record indicating that he hadn't let go of the Lucifer Rising soundtrack dispute. Anger's salvo of caustic energy seems to have stunted JP's creative growth and seal him into a permanent stasis of sorts. We'll never know for sure but it's rather curious, don't you think?

It's common knowledge that Jimmy Page is very keen on a reunion tour. John Paul Jones, ever the passive one, would surely be aboard.

However, the self-professed golden god Robert Plant is a rock block, if you will. Ever since Plant's tragedy he's been in the driver's seat when it comes to the direction of the band. He could take it or leave it and has all the control because there's no way they could do the band's legacy any justice without all three remaining members involved. Interestingly enough, once Robert Plant distanced himself a bit from Led Zeppelin he cultivated a successful solo career and has been by all accounts very happy. Why?

Plant often gets snippy when journalists ask him about another tour as Zeppelin. It's been estimated that a reunion could bring in over a billion dollars! Plant goes on about how he doesn't want to be a 'jukebox' and that stadium rock on this level is overly commercialized soul-robbing rubbish, etc. Sure, he's got plenty of money and is in a much better position financially than many of the old bands from the 70's and 80's replenishing their bank accounts with nostalgia tours. However, these are not the real reasons he doesn't want to tour as Zeppelin again. And touring specifically as Zeppelin is a very important detail. Why?

There is a telling clue here and it's related to one of the (many) sputtering almost-reunions the band had. Zeppelin got back together for the

1985 Live Aid benefit concert in Philadelphia. There wasn't much time to rehearse and it was a decidedly poor performance but Plant said he was drunk on it all and missed the rush of singing in front of a huge audience. It was such a feeling that they soon began rehearsing again but it all started falling apart after a couple of weeks as tension among them grew and they began to get on each other's nerves.

Then it happened. Their stand-in drummer Tony Thompson (formerly of the band Chic) was involved in a minor car accident while being driven home from the pub one night. Apparently, this was seen as an omen by Plant. Remember of course that his 1975 car crash was the unofficial inception point of the Led Zeppelin Curse.

After Thompson's fender-bender Plant began to question the whole endeavor saying that nobody wanted to hear that old stuff again, etc. However, this completely contradicted the general consensus that, in fact, everyone wanted to see Zeppelin get back together. That particular failed reunion attempt is key because Plant's apprehension, specifically triggered by a car accident, was indicative that he knew something was stalking Zeppelin. That little spurt of bad luck brought him back in time, back to the heavy fog that enveloped the band and took Zeppelin down. Plant was spooked and the reunion was scrapped.

I think that playing the old music together for any longer than a single engagement scares Plant and for good reason. He's done one-off performances for worthy causes (such as the aforementioned Live Aid concert) or for special occasions like tributes, etc. but has either refused to do a full-on reunion tour or when one was in the works it fell apart when he balked. I think he misses performing as Zeppelin but doesn't want to pull that dark pocket of time forward into the now and I don't blame him.

I won't go into the specifics of brief Zeppelin reformations and reunion tour chatter that never amounted to anything because it's all over the internet. In fact, it's torturous for diehard fans because there's so much 'yes its happening, not it's not' talk out there that you wonder if the Curse itself is behind all of this. It's such a tease and always ends up in a let-down which just rubs salt into the wound.

Jimmy Page and John Paul Jones don't need the money and it's obvious they want to have fun and relive the 70's; play their old music and maybe some new stuff and just have a blast. Not Plant though and from the public's perspective he appears to be an old stick in the mud about it. However, to be fair, there's some scary stuff he'd rather not reconstitute.

Some scabs you just shouldn't pick at. We'll never know the full story but I can assure you that the thing he won't risk awakening, even for a billion dollar payday, is pretty intense. Jimmy Page on the other hand is willing to open Pandora's Box. This is because whatever has gotten its hooks into him is making life more uncomfortable now than what he remembers from the late 70's. He'll gladly take that risk to experience the old rush and get some relief from the ache of the curse.

So the reunion rumors continue and occasionally Plant and Page get snitty with each other via the media over whether or not they'll get back together. In my opinion this is (at least in part) due to the Curse emerging from its lair and tearing yet another chunk of flesh off the carcass that is Led Zeppelin. Kenneth Anger, at the time of this writing still ticking along at ninety, is watching from afar as the curse creature does his bidding. Ok; maybe a bit dramatic but as I mentioned earlier, levity keeps the demonic at bay and this is pretty creepy stuff when you really think about it. So who or what is ultimately responsible for this Curse?

8 Conclusions and Culpability

We've gone over Led Zeppelin's descent which resulted in John Bonham's death and the end of the original incarnation of the band. Also covered were the post-Zeppelin/Bonham years and the curse's effect on what was left of the group. Could all of this bad luck just be due to general life circumstances; stuff that can happen to anyone and was just magnified by Zeppelin's fame and Jimmy Page's innocuous occult hobby? But then again, maybe the accidents and deaths were karma or payback related to an alleged deal the band made with nefarious, invisible forces? Or did Kenneth Anger's Curse of King Midas seal Zeppelin's fate? As I've said all along, it's impossible to prove either way as this is all very subjective. But of course I'm going to share my opinion...and it's just that, an opinion.

This definitely isn't a black or white issue and I'll have to delve into another band's history to make my case. Before Kenneth Anger met Jimmy Page he was involved with The Rolling Stones. Anger's conversations with lead singer Mick Jagger allegedly inspired the song Sympathy for the Devil which was released in December of 1968. The infernal song was also inspired by the Russian novel The Master and Margarita as Jagger was into all sorts of occult literature in the late sixties.

Many have spoken of this period as being the Stones' demonic phase which sounds appropriately labeled and was certainly fed by their association with Anger. It proved to be fertile ground for the filmmaker and occultist to work his magick on the band. In addition to Jagger, Anger was close to his girlfriend Marianne Faithfull, Stones guitarists Brian Jones and Keith Richards and also their (at different times) girlfriend German-Italian model and film star Anita Pallenberg.

The Stones' were interested in the occult as it was hip at the time and being rock stars they leaned towards the dark side. Anger worked with the band wherever his occult or film interests could find common ground. Jagger recorded the score for his short movie Invocation of My Demon Brother (1969) and then Jagger and Faithfull got involved in Anger's film Lucifer Rising. Of course this is the long-term project that Jimmy Page later committed to composing the score for. Before JP got involved, Jagger was at various times to either do the score or play the lead part but it all ended when he decided to pull out.

Anger had also become quite fixated on Brian Jones and believed that he and Pallenberg were witches. Jones had allegedly shown Anger an 'extra nipple' he had on his thigh which the filmmaker said would have been perceived as a mark of the Devil in Medieval times. Jones was fired from the band in June of 1969 for drug problems and was soon found dead in his swimming pool under mysterious circumstances. In December of 1969 the Stones performed in a free concert at the Altamont Speedway in Northern California. This event became known as the Altamont tragedy which claimed several lives and resulted in an array of injuries and destruction.

In addition, Anger lived for a short time with Richards and Pallenberg. He was to officiate their wedding in Pagan fashion but

Richards ended up calling off the ceremony and kicking Anger out. Why? Anger took doors of their home off the hinges and painted them gold; the color of Satan's aura as per magickal teachings according to the filmmaker. Needless to say this freaked the couple out. Years later, Anger claims not to remember this incident but as you can see, he walked a fine line in his dealings with the Rolling Stones. They were intrigued by the danger and excitement of the occult and I'm sure they knew what it did for their image with young fans but Anger ultimately took it too far. It's apparent that whenever Kenneth Anger gets involved with a band things seem to go awry.

I share all of this to draw a parallel between Kenneth Anger's connection to rock music and how it leads to death, destruction and general bad vibes. I believe that rock can (not always but certainly often) be a delivery mechanism for astral energies (spirits, demons, etc.) and people like Anger are the third dimensional facilitators or conduits for this. That is another story altogether and no, I'm not an evangelical nut. I don't judge these otherworldly beings, their vessels (such as Anger) or their alleged agendas in any way shape or form. I'm just fascinated by how it all comes about and manifests in the physical world.

Conclusions and Culpability

My conclusion is that due to Kenneth Anger's pattern of involvement with the rock music world his collaboration with Jimmy Page did indeed create the Led Zeppelin Curse. I'm quite sure he would be proud of this conclusion. I don't judge the man or anyone involved with him as their interactions are by choice whether consciously or not. It's all a journey; all experience and nothing to label good, bad, evil or what have you.

As we previously discussed, the main series of Zeppelin's public bad luck started with Robert Plant's car accident in 1975 but that was before Anger's Curse of King Midas on Jimmy Page. I think Anger's general involvement with Page starting in 1971 began a slow buildup of chaos energy and the dam began to crack and ultimately broke with the 1975 car crash. His curse after being ejected from Jimmy Page's home in 1976 just expedited what was already happening energetically with the band due to his earlier involvement. It was all downhill for Zeppelin from there.

Fame and all that comes with it draws in massive amounts of psychic energy and those who seek to get close to the famous get a hit, if you will, of that juice and it can become addictive. People that know how to harness and manipulate psychic vibrations, people like

Kenneth Anger, can tap into the pool of energy that rock stars like Zeppelin have around them and use it as a sort of fuel; akin to vampirism. Anger was very clever in this regard but he may not have been fully conscious of what he was doing. Sure, he intended the curse but the long term energy drain connected to Page's creative inertia and inability to tour as Zeppelin again may have been covertly orchestrated by the demonic forces around him.

Although it may appear that I'm painting Anger as the villain this is not the case. What is Star Wars without Darth Vader? Would Lord of the Rings be any fun without Sauron? What I'm getting at here is that Kenneth Anger was serving a cosmic purpose in the dance of life. Without conflict we learn nothing. Humans evolve through cause and effect and Kenneth Anger's (as well as Aleister Crowley's) insertion into Jimmy Page's orbit was a necessary part of his personal growth.

I would even cautiously venture to suggest that Zeppelin would not be the mega-legend they are today without Anger's injection of caustic energy. I know that will seem blasphemous to some of you but this theory cannot be proven or disproven. There are innumerable alternate realities and maybe in the one where Kenneth Anger doesn't exist, the original lineup of Zeppelin (including Bonham) are travelling the nostalgia concert circuit. Maybe history would have lumped them in with their less successful contemporaries?

Was Jimmy Page in some way responsible for the curse? Did he practice black magick? Personally, I don't think he made any pact with the Devil or performed black magick rituals. How one defines these rituals is another matter though. Some consider any sort of a ceremony in which one seeks to commune with and/or benefit from nonphysical agents 'black magick'. I don't agree with that at all.

However, JP did reprint the demonic Goetia conjuring book through his Equinox store and I can't imagine that he didn't at one time or another try to summon and converse with the entities from this ancient manual. It's utterly fascinating and irresistible for young occultists to throw caution to the wind and knock on that door. But I think JP was just experimenting and maybe sought to bring good fortune to the band through these energies. The catch is that demons always want something in return.

Playing with Goetia, even without any malevolent intent, would have drawn in a plethora of nasty energies which I'm sure swirled around the band. But once again, Anger's involvement was like repeatedly dumping a bucket of gasoline onto a small campfire. In the end, I don't think Jimmy Page meant to harm anyone through his experimentation. He's indirectly culpable, at best, for the Led Zeppelin Curse. But then again, aren't we all? Isn't life just one grand experiment?

Although I do feel that Kenneth Anger is the lynchpin to this curse, an interesting connection between Jimmy Page, Aleister Crowley and Anger has emerged. Both Page and Anger are devotees of Crowley. This of course isn't that big a deal as many, many people are Crowleyites to varying degrees. But let's watch as this trinity becomes more tightly focused.

Then we have Crowley owning and practicing intense rituals in Boleskine House. Kenneth Anger later inhabits this same house for a period of time and undoubtedly also performs occult ceremonies there. Very shortly thereafter Jimmy Page buys Boleskine House; owning it for almost twenty two years. Say what you will but he assuredly performed magick in that home as well.

All three men living (at various times) in the same house and performing rituals on the premises fuses their energies. This carries over and inextricably links each one's destiny as well.

I would even venture to say that all three are karmically connected; if you believe in that sort of thing. They were all on similar evolutionary trajectories and met (whether energetically and/or physically) at various junctures in various ways directly affecting the others' personal journeys through time.

But I'm not finished as we also have the Abbey of Thelema connection. Crowley's occultic debaucheries in Sicily created a beacon of sorts which both Anger and Page responded to by visiting the haunted sex barn years later. We know that Anger performed rituals there and as for Page; well your guess is as good as mine.

The final connection in this infernal triad (sorry, I couldn't help it) is of course the Led Zeppelin Curse itself. Anger and Page fatefully met at an auction of Crowley memorabilia which set them on a collision course resulting in the legend we are exploring right now. Magick has a way of doing that. I'm not saying this is the case each and every time people are introduced via the mysterious workings of the occult but I've definitely noticed that these relationships often go sour at some point. But then again, perhaps this is just my own personal connection with magick and the smudged lens I'm viewing it through.

Yes; this Page, Crowley and Anger connection is just a theory and by now you know that I'm full of such conjecture. However; theories are brave and what would we have without them? So-called facts are safe and familiar but we often forget that facts are born of theories and without such bold stretches we'd live in a world that was boring and too comfortable which is paradoxically very dangerous.

9 Boleskine House– Paranormal Vortex

As discussed in the preface, on December 23rd, 2015 it was reported that Boleskine House was ablaze and by the time fire crews had arrived approximately 60% of the structure was already destroyed. The owners at the time of the fire were Dutch and used the place as a holiday home. Their daughter and her partner were there and had reportedly come back from the shops to find the house in flames. The initial report was that the fire started in the kitchen and was not thought to be set deliberately but then again how do you define deliberate? In chapter two we discussed the fire that burned down the 10th century church with (allegedly) the entire congregation inside. This is why I said earlier that the story begins and ends with fire.

There has been some online chatter about the timeline of the blaze in relation to photos that were taken as the house was burning. The vantage point of the photographer was called into question arousing suspicions of arson. If true, it could have been insurance related or perhaps connected to the droves of Crowley and Page acolytes that make the pilgrimage to this house of the unholy.

It had been reported that up to six fire engines and thirty firefighters were battling the blaze. So was it the Devil that lit the fire? Was it arson in an attempt to cash in on insurance? There was also rumor that the house was going up for sale soon. Maybe it was just a plain old electrical fire with no boogeyman about? Does it really matter? The bottom line is that the place burned down and I'm of the opinion that the residual occult energy is the cause.

Even if it's proven that the fire was intentionally lit or that it was just an electrical fault is irrelevant. The ghosts that have been there since the beginning (churches are not built in specific places by accident) had their way and decided it was time for a cleansing. The most common (and completely untraceable) effect of entity involvement in 3D physical world affairs is the old mental prompt or as I call it 'impulsing'.

So let's say that the spirits or demons (or whatever you want to call them) wanted a fire they would connect with someone who lived in the house or had access to the property and set off a chain reaction of impulsing which would result in a fire. This could take the form of an accident such as falling asleep with a cigarette or leaving the stove/oven on or the fireplace lit, etc. Name your 'accident' and entities can make it happen via a human vessel.

Let's say it was an electrical fault. Now I won't go as far to suggest that the electrician was impulsed into wiring things incorrectly but in this case entities can produce electrical charges of their own from beyond the veil. These charges of otherworldly origin could interfere with the physical electrical wiring and then bam, there's your fire. Yes; it's all untraceable and un-provable but I've been involved with this stuff long enough to know how it can happen. If you've made it this far into the book I trust you value my opinion.

So at the time of this writing the charred rubble of Boleskine House is fenced off and who knows what will come of the property. Will the remaining structure be completely razed and rebuilt exactly as before or will a new structure take its place? Regardless of what happens, something will be built on that prime piece of property by the Loch and then the spirits will come up from the land and infest the new structure; it's inevitable.

Crowley, Boleskine House and Jimmy Page may very well be a small part of an even bigger story here. Due to Crowley basically tearing a gaping hole in the astral plane and quite possibly the fabric of time itself with his exciting yet irresponsible occult misadventure there has been whisper of a connection between AC and Nessie, the famed Loch Ness Monster.

I suspect a good many of you had the knee-jerk reaction of thinking this is absolute rubbish but hear me out. After all, you've come this far, right? So how is it that Aleister Crowley and the Loch Ness Monster are both infamous for working their own unique brands of magic in the same place? Is it just a coincidence or is there anything about the area itself that might be responsible for these two seemingly unconnected supernatural legends?

As you know, the land Boleskine House stands on has quite a history. We referenced the ancient kirk (church) that burned down with the congregation still inside and then the 17th century minister who had to lay the bodies of the undead back to rest after a local wizard had summoned them from Boleskine graveyard. Then there is the Lord Lovat execution which occurred at the Tower in London yet it's allegedly his rolling head which used to haunt Boleskine House nightly. We also have the deaths and mayhem connected to Crowley and of course the Led Zeppelin Curse which connects through Jimmy Page's ownership of the now charred lakeside manor.

However, the Scottish Highlands have long had their myths, folklore and legends. The Kelpie is a mythical water horse that was said to haunt Scotland's lochs and rivers. It seems the Kelpie would appear to it's victims as a pony and entice them to ride on its back before taking them to a watery grave. Selkies, another type of mythical creature, could supposedly transform themselves from seal to human and then back again. I'm sure you can see where this is going. Then we have Scotland's most famous mythical creature, the Loch Ness Monster; old Nessie herself. So what's the Crowley connection?

It's been suggested that AC may have accidentally summoned the Loch Ness monster with his botched ritual. The timelines seem to match up which we'll discuss in a moment but I don't think he summoned Nessie so much as created the conditions for more consistent manifestation of the creature on the physical plane.

Loch Ness is approximately 23 miles long and over 1 mile wide. Have a look at it online…it resembles a vagina, doesn't it? Where am I going with this? Well, it seems that the area has 'birthed' a lot of phenomena. Loch Ness lies in the Great Glen fault line between Fort Augustus and Inverness and is the longest glen in Scotland. The Great Glen is a large side-slip fault line which is active and splits the north of Scotland down the middle. Large cavities in the earth such as this are often linked to paranormal activity and are considered by indigenous peoples and mystics to be portals to the inner earth or even other realities.

Now Aleister Crowley certainly didn't create Nessie because the earliest report of a monster in the vicinity of Loch Ness appears in The Life of St. Columbia, written in the 7th century. Other sightings include one from the 1870's but a sharp increase of Nessie reports began in 1933 which is about twenty years after Aleister Crowley sold Boleskine house and this also coincides with the beginning of Crowley's downfall.

In 1934 Crowley was declared bankrupt after trying to sue an artist who called him a black magician. Ah; defamation of character!

This ridiculous attempt to secure short term funds backfired on the old wizard as the judge was utterly appalled at what came up during the trial about Crowley's life and activities. I guess the prude couldn't handle mention of black magick, orgies and bestiality.

After the law suit Crowley descended into heroin addiction (i.e. the demons completely took over) and eventually died of a respiratory infection at age 72. Curiously enough, there are exactly 72 demons in the Goetia spell book that both Crowley and Jimmy Page were so fond of. Another interesting aside is that on the day of Crowley's death he demanded a dose of heroin from his doctor who refused. At least he had more integrity than Michael Jackson's doctor. Crowley then cursed the physician who supposedly died within 24 hours. Wow; one last win for the Great Beast!

Ok; back to the Loch Ness Monster. So from 1933 onward the Nessie legend grew. There were seemingly credible reports and then there were the outright hoaxes. Unfortunately, hoaxes tarnish all of the potentially legit sightings in the eyes of skeptics. Now the Loch Ness Monster is mainly a souvenir shop side note bringing tourist revenue into the Highlands...or is it?

There is a theory that Nessie is more of a supernatural creature as opposed to a flat-out physical being like you and I. This take on the legend has its pros and cons in regards to credibility. Due to all of the sonar sweeping done in the loch to prove/disprove the monster's existence, anomalies came up which indicated that perhaps the creature knew how to conceal itself or phased in and out of physical reality. The skeptics will call this pseudoscience rationalization whereas the parapsychologists, ghost hunters and crypto-zoologists will exclaim 'of course!'

I think there are a number of variables which make Loch Ness a perfect storm of paranormal and occult phenomena. As previously discussed, reports of strange creatures in this area date as far back as 565! The idea that the Nessies (there seem to be more than one) are supernatural creatures fits in very well with the ancient lore and also the circumstances around more recent sightings. These creatures may not be flesh and blood in the sense that they can be physically touched but nevertheless can be seen with the human eye.

There are many places throughout the world where paranormal activity consistently occurs and quite often these places are supposedly along ley lines. Ley lines are said to make up an energy grid of sorts around the earth which can amplify or create the necessary conditions for supernatural phenomena. Paranormal researchers have plotted ley lines around Loch Ness which could very well be a factor in these sightings. If you add the variable of the Great Glen fault line and its energy this could increase the chances for otherworldly creatures like Nessie to slip through the veil into the physical world. However, there is one last ingredient to our perfect storm.

The intense and elaborate ritual that Aleister Crowley conducted at Boleskine House most certainly was a factor in creating a little tear in the fabric of space-time. However, by not banishing the forces he summoned, that little tear became an irreversible rip allowing astral beings to come and go as they please.

Where does Jimmy Page fit in? First of all, who knows what rituals he performed at Boleskine House. All we hear is that there were lavish 'parties' (rituals?) and he otherwise spent 'very little' time there. Then we have the Page loyalists who say they never saw him perform any ceremonies and that he was just an occult 'researcher'.

First of all, I very seriously doubt that JP didn't perform any rituals at Boleskine House.

I'm not saying he did Black Masses or sacrificed animals/people but he most certainly did magick there. Secondly, just the fact that Jimmy Page owned Boleskine House and Led Zeppelin fans knew he was into the occult definitely magnetized additional energy to the property thus fortifying what the Great Glen and Crowley had started.

Fame and the collective mental focus (i.e. energy) that it draws is very powerful. This is part of the reason why so many celebrities are unstable and/or substance abusers. Think about all of the vibes coming at them from people watching their movies, listening to their music and/or reading tabloids, etc. If we can accept that radio signals invisibly, wirelessly travel from their point of origin and make music come out of our radios then why can't the transmissions of the most powerful device of all (the human mind) reach and have an effect on their intended receivers? Anyway; the vibes coming from Zeppelin fans definitely added to the potency of the vortex in Boleskine House and the surrounding area.

I saved the best hypothesis for last. Is Jimmy Page possessed by Aleister Crowley? Real possession is not spinning heads and projectile pea soup. It's far more insidious and common than you might think. I wrote about this extensively in my last book. There are any number of ways that this possession could have occurred. Think about it; you've got two people owning the same house in different time periods where dark occult rituals occurred and in an overall area (surrounding Loch Ness) that is known for paranormal phenomena. Crowley's energy, his very essence, is in that property and here comes a guy who admired him and practiced elements (at the very least) of his magick and philosophy. That's a strong resonance. Then add all of the sex and drugs (from both) and there you have the ultimate recipe for possession.

Once again, Kenneth Anger's influence comes into play as well. Although JP's music wasn't used in Lucifer Rising the guitarist does make a cameo in the film. In that scene we see a bearded Jimmy Page staring at a wreathed portrait of Aleister Crowley while holding an Egyptian stele which is a stone or wooden slab used for funerary or commemorative purposes. It's as if JP was staring into a mirror and he became Crowley.

Mirror magick is potent and dangerous. The Goetia, a spell book that Crowley definitely used and Jimmy Page liked enough to (at the very least) reprint with great care, utilizes a mirror for the evocation of demonic entities. Was

Kenneth Anger sending a message with that scene? Was he setting Page up somehow? Anger has stated that his films are rituals unto themselves. This image from the film can be found online- have a look. In addition to his very public Curse of King Midas, Anger might have helped facilitate the grafting of Aleister Crowley's consciousness onto JP's energy field via this film/ritual.

There doesn't have to be a dramatic shift in personality for possession to take place. It could be a cohabitation of sorts that JP wouldn't even be aware of. For those of you that don't believe in magick or the occult (and that's perfectly understandable if you haven't experienced it) this will sound utterly ridiculous. But to the believers this will sound like the ultimate ritual. Think about it- the dead magician entering the young, rich and famous rock star's body to once again enjoy the pleasures of the flesh. Whichever side you fall on, it's interesting stuff to consider.

In the end we don't know what really happened. It will be forever open to debate. Is there a Zeppelin Curse and if so, was it Jimmy Page's dabbling or Kenneth Anger's malevolent salvo of spite that caused the group's bad luck? Was it even bad luck or just life taking its course and people creating something where there's nothing as they so often do. Humanity loves drama and the internet just fuels and amplifies it.

The only way to learn new things and create exciting journeys is to stay open and never assume anything or become hardwired to a particular viewpoint or doctrine. I believe the Led Zeppelin Curse is real but then again what is real? For me the goal was exploring the subject matter and travelling down the various paths that it created. The story isn't over...it never is, right?

The next installment in this series will focus on Boleskine House itself and the stories from locals about Jimmy Page, Aleister Crowley and whether or not Nessie is somehow connected. I'll travel to Inverness Scotland and bring you along too by documenting the adventure with onsite podcasts and even a journey beneath the icy waters of Loch Ness.

I'll see you there...

41816615R00107

Made in the USA
San Bernardino, CA
05 July 2019